All rights reserved. No part of this publication may be reproduced or transmitted in any form or by any means, electronic or mechanical, including photocopy, recording, or any information storage and retrieval system, without permission in writing from Todd Kachinski Kottmeier.

ISBN-13:
978-1724512499

ISBN-10:
1724512498
Copyright © 2015 and 2018 Todd Kachinski

SECOND EDITION

DRAG411's Ten Black Books

Book 1:	**DRAG411's "DRAG Bully, A Survivor's Guide"**
	Copyright © 2015 and 2018
Book 2:	**DRAG411's "Original DRAG Handbook"**
	Copyright © 2010, 2011, 2012, 2014, and 2018
Book 3:	**DRAG411's "Crown Me! Winning Pageants"**
	Copyright © 2013, 2014, and 2018
Book 4:	**DRAG411's "DRAG King Handbook"**
	Copyright © 2014 and 2018
Book 5:	**DRAG411's "DRAG Stories"**
	Copyright © 2011, 2014, and 2018
Book 6:	**DRAG411's "DRAG Mother, DRAG Father"**
	Copyright © 2012, 2014, and 2018
Book 7:	**DRAG411's "SPOTLIGHT TODAY"**
	Copyright © 2012 and 2018
Book 8:	**DRAG411's "DRAG Queen Guide"**
	Copyright © 2014 and 2018
Book 9:	Two Comedy Scripts:
	DRAG411's "Best Said Dead"
	Copyright © 2011, 2014, and 2018
	"Following Wynter"
	Copyright © 2012, 2014, and 2018
Book 10:	**DRAG411's "DRAG World"**
	Copyright © 2012 and 2018

From the best-selling author of "CommUnity of Transition,"
"Two Days Past Dead," The Novel and the sequel,
"Turn Around Bright Eyes, The DRAG Queen Killer,"
"Joey Brooks, The Show Must Go On,"
And "Waiting On God."

DRAG411's

DRAG Bully
A Survivor's Guide

2nd Edition

I am not a fan of the term "drag" as applied across this entire art form, but until they find a single word "more accepting," I will have to use it. The drag community has helped me earn twenty LGBT world records. I created DRAG411 to document this form of entertainment. We are the world's largest organization for male, female, and androgynous impersonators with over 7,000 current or former impersonators in 32 countries.   The Infamous Todd Kachinski Kottmeier

About Todd Kachinski

DRAG BULLY is my 25th book, 20th World record, and 12th DRAG411 resource guide. Often helping others "helps you." I want to thank all of you for helping me over the years to document the lives of people around you through all my projects as a historian and author. I hope that we helped change the world together; I know all of you have successfully changed me.

DRAG411 is the largest organization for impersonators in the world with over 7,000 members in 32 countries. Its Memorial wall alone is the largest and oldest listing of entertainers now performing on a grander stage. Check us out at DRAG411.comThis will be the last compilation book of my life. I promised before my dementia got worse that I would take the words on bullying, shared by over a hundred entertainers and get it into print. There will be no more new DRAG411 books. Just writing those words have tears in my eyes. I have to believe part of them is from the emotions of knowing I accomplished the last book. It took a little longer, but because of the wonderful people in my life, it is now finished heading to the printer.

The Term "DRAG"

Lost in History

DR.A.G does not appear until the 20th century. However, we often incorrectly credit Shakespeare. During his time, females in England could perform onstage, so men "**dr**essed **a**s **g**irls," which people believed represented the word drag. Zero references in any of Shakespeare's writing support this acronym or reference. Actually, the term has no written record of usage prior to the First World War Personally, I am not a fan of the term, but until "everyone" can agree on a better term... we are stuck with it.

Editor's Note

More than 100 people contributed to developing and answering the questions that comprise the chapters of this book. We chose the best, most comprehensive, insightful, or most common. To all of the contributing writers, we owe a debt of gratitude for the thousands of words donated to help inspire, motivate, and show a world, "they are not alone." We asked thousands of male, female, and androgynous impersonators to send us anonymous words of wisdom to share on these topics. We did not place credit to each sentence crediting each entertainer for a reason. Often when people get mad at someone, they ignore even their helpful advice. We needed someone bullied to understand the wisdom, untethered by preconceived attitudes. Sometimes the person you may dislike the most, survived the exact same situation. DRAG BULLY is about survival; its words donated without conditional support by performers, including:

AJ Menendez
Alana Chapelle
Alexandra Bond
Amy DeMilo
Anastacia Rose
Anastasia C Principle
Anita Rivera
Ashl Farrington
Ashton "the origin8r"
Aurora Lee Richards
B. Louise
Bad Karma
Barbie Dayne
Bo Micheals.
Britney Towers
Cadillac Monroe
Carnita K Asada
Cathy Craig

Celia Cruz
Chad Michaels
Cherish D'men Dupri
Christina Jackson
Dee Gregory
Devin Deluca
Dexter
Dexter Maine-Love
Dionysus W Khaos
E.M. Shaun
Eartha Quake
Esmé Rodríguez
Freddy Prinze Charming
Gia GiaVanni
Glitz Glam
Harrie Bradshaw
Harry Pi
Jade Iroq
Jasper Nova
Jayda Clyne
Joey Brooks
Johnny Angel
Kamen Cider
Kay Starr
Kendra Blake
Kenya C. McCooter
Keyun Starr
Klawn Oppun
Kody Sky
Kody Wellch Klondyke
Kristofer V. Lee
Kruz Mhee
Lady Anya Face
Lady Davona
Lana Towers
Le Kross DeAire
Luke Ateraz
Madison Avinew
Martina Marraccino

Maxine Padlock/Maxi PAD
Melodie Renée Sommers
Misty Boxx
Mya Lamour
Myami Richards
Naomi Fiercee
Natasha Richards
Nikki Newman
Nostalgia Todd Ronin
Osiris Diazz
Persian Prince
Rasta Boi Punany
Rico M Taylor
River DeAire'
Rylee Ray Prettyman
Samantha St. Clair
Saoirse Glam
Sapphire d'Syre
Sasha Stephens
Sertraline Del Mar
ShaeShae LaReese
Sonny D
Trudy Tyler
Tula
Ty DeCon
Tyler T Roll
Tyra Marie
Valexa Blu
Vanity Van Dank
Victoria Valkyries
Vinnie Marconi
Vita Krawford
Wynter Storm
Zekira Zabertini

DRAG411.com　　　　　　　The 10 Black Books, Book 1

(sic)

Latin adverb: thus"; in full: sic erat scriptum, thus was it written indicates DRAG411 transcribed the comments into this book exactly as found in the original source, complete with any erroneous or archaic spelling or other nonstandard presentation. We try to print the responses using the same words sent to us, ensuring the reader DRAG411 did not change the tone, reflection, or character of each response.

We print verbatim, without editing

ver·ba·tim　　　　　vərˈbātəm/
adverb: verbatim; adjective
in exactly the same words as used originally.

(sic)

Go to our website at
Drag411.com
to locate any name listed
in any of the books
in our Ten Black Book series
and the details of each
book, entertainer,
and chapter.

Chapters of Survival

Chapter One
"Friends"

Chapter Two
"Neighbors"

Chapter Three
"Peers"

Chapter Four
"First Date"

Chapter Five
"Relationships"

Chapter Six
"Employment"

Chapter Seven
"Family"

Chapter Eight
"Patrons"

Chapter Nine
"Self-doubt"

Chapter Ten
"Last Words of Wisdom"

I dedicate hundreds of hours placed in this book to

DRAG411

I created DRAG411 years ago to develop a safe place for impersonators to share their voices, wisdom, and experience. In time, many books and projects became reality, and over 7,000 entertainers actively participated in 32 countries. Because of them, and hopefully because of you, I know have twenty LGBT world titles. The DRAG411 project that started it all, is the "Original, Official DRAG Handbook." Many of the contributors of the Original, Official DRAG Handbook and so many other DRAG411 books are no longer with us.

The Infamous Todd Kachinski Kottmeier

> "Positive, constructive help is not the same as criticism. One offers the chance to repair while the other offers the chance to destroy."
> Todd Kachinski Kottmeier

Chapter One

❀❀❀

How do you get past friends knocking you down because you either do drag or believe you are not good at drag?

Note: To maintain the integrity of this project, I did not edit most of the postings to allow the message sent in, to be in the actual words of the impersonator. I left them anonymous to allow the reader to understand them without pre-conceived bias.

❀

I sat down with each of them, one by one. I made sure they were the only conversation in the room. I told them, "If you are my friend, truly a friend… you will support me even if I thought I could be an astronaut. True friends encourage their friends to follow their dreams. At the end of the conversation, either I had someone in my corner or I realized this person perhaps was never a friend at all. Never confuse a true friend with "the truth." True friends may tell you the truth when they say 'you are a mess." Challenge them to help you become better. True friends will sit by you as you learn the craft. Promise me, few performers look back at the photos of their early years and whisper to themselves, "I was the perfect from day one."

❀

Friends often state, "My drag is not good enough or does not involve enough change." Perhaps they have evolving or they are worth more and their fans love them in the world of popularity. I have found that for me, I have to believe truly in myself, to be confident in what I do and in what type of entertainment I am projecting. I grow as other entertainers do, but we may all do so at a different pace. Some excel faster than others do, but I have to stay true to myself and keep on pushing. Always continue to redefine and provide the best possible me.

❀

Remove all negative people from your life. They will only bring you down.

❀

It took a while for me to realize why I loved it so much. Once I did, I felt no need to explain myself. Instead, I surrounded myself with like-minded people whose advice and help was beneficial to my career as a female impersonator. Drag impersonators are not trying to be women. They are merely acting and entertainment. Other trans* people like me, who enjoy showing our accomplishments as such thru competition and entertainment.
*Trans refers to transgender, transsexual, transitioning…

I try to keep my head up high. I watch videos of my performances so I can improve as an entertainer. I always tell myself, "as long as you stay true to yourself, you will carry on"

❀

You do what makes you happy. As long as you are happy with what you are doing, and quality of the work you produce. Then fuck them all. They are just jealous

❀

My friends told me, "I was too big, not good on my feet, and other comments long lost in memories best stored away." I wanted to prove them wrong. I needed to believe I was stronger as a person than the words they selected to share with me. I look back now at my life. I have worked Vegas and stages around the world. What have they done with their lives? I have photos, boxes and cases, and tubs and totes of the most spectacular moments of my life. Never let other people define the person you shall become. You control that power in your life; seize it, revel in its glory.

❀

Never told, "you are not good at drag." I have received from relatives or others that do not believe in it, "why do you do it?" I reply, "Why do boxers fight to get the lights knocked out of them, or why dancers, dance?" It is simply an "out" for me. For decades, people use music for expression not necessarily, because I want to be a dude, hell I do not even typically wear facial hair. I do it simply to express myself for the entertainment of others. It takes guts, or balls of you want to call it that. Yes, first time I went onstage I puked as soon as I walked off, because of the fear of, what did they think about me? Did I look like a goon? I had confidence in myself. Soon I had people reaching out to me, of how great they thought I was, and I began receiving request. Eight years later, I am proud to say, I am somewhat of a staple in our small Birmingham community and I have done some traveling. I never forget the reason I started performing; I simply wanted to express myself, and bring smiles to my audience.

❀

I just am myself. I listen though when they think I am not good.

❀

You have to ignore them or realize that they are not true friends. Keep working at finding your own original stage persona and be faithful to your vision.

❀

Remember why you do this; it makes you happy and it makes others happy. Most of the time negative words just come from a lack of understanding. Let them know how happy it makes you. Your true friends will take the time to understand and will stand by you.

❀

Stayed focused on the positives not the negatives; always, no matter what.

❦

You did not start this journey for them, so their support is not required. Find the people who do support you and stick with them. Keep an open mind for constructive criticism, but do not let anybody with a bad word or bad eyebrows tell you shit.

❦

If you have friends who do not support you doing drag, then they are not truly your friends. True friends support each other in whatever adventures and hobbies we choose. If your friends are saying, you are not good at it and you know it is not because they do not want you to do it, ask them why they feel that way. They might be seeing something that you are not. They might be the only ones who are stepping forward and speaking the truth. Not all of us are cutout to be drag performers. I would rather have friends who are open and honest about something like that than ones who falsely encourage me when I am actually doing a bad job.

❦

I remind them, everyone has something they do that they love they may not be good at but that does not mean they should not do it. One day, they will need support and may want to rethink how they treat people or there will be no one left to do so.

❦

I am blessed with an amazing group of friends that just happen to be drag impersonators. This is the best thing to do, as I am entertained. Surround yourself with people who can help you become a better performer and will support you no matter what.

❦

I have been very blessed in this regard. If they made negative comments, I have either entirely ignored or not heard such remarks. I know I can be so much better; so I do believe there are detractors out there.

❦

I continue improving myself to prove them wrong or I will tell them to try to do better. No friends have actually knocked me just for doing drag.

❦

It is all about why you are doing drag. If you are doing it for other people, you are going to let them get to you. If you are doing drag for yourself, no one can bring you down. I do it for me, and so I do not let things get to me.

❦

I keep myself surrounded with positive people. I do not let negativity into my life.

❦

I have been very lucky to have a group of friends who have not only been supportive, but encouraging. When I told people I wanted to do drag but not shave my beard, there were a few confused reactions. Once I performed in my first show, it seemed to click with people. You have to own the entertainer you want to be. P!nk is one my idols and I remember an interview where she said, "I am the impersonator of fuck it." I like to live by that philosophy.

❀

For me personally, I feel like the first two steps include. "Understanding yourself and why you want to be a part of drag." When you have a goal and you are passionate about it, it can be very difficult for naysayers to discourage you. I love the feeling on being onstage and the level of self-expression it gives me. I hold that very near and dear and it is what pushes me even when others around me chose not to share my passion.

❀

Words can hurt. To get past the things people say, I would listen at first but remind myself of who is the one onstage. When I am performing, I am expressing myself; nobody else can do me. Unless it is constructive or helpful, people's words would not push me forward as a performer. I do not linger on them.

❀

I try to focus on bettering myself as an entertainer. If someone puts me down, I use the anger and frustration inside me as a driving force to say "You are wrong about me, I am worthy and I will not allow you to tell me otherwise." Everyone is entitled to his or her own opinion. Not every opinion is right or true.

❀

People who do not support you are not your friends.

❀

I do my best not to listen to the negativity even though it is hard to do. If a friend is knocking you down, they are not a friend. Friends should support you. Words only have power if you give you give them power so always listen to the positivity and drown out the negativity!

❀

I start surrounding myself with different people or ask them how I can do it better? I even challenge them to do what I do.

❀

My friends were actually supportive because it makes me happy. If they cannot support your happiness, they do not deserve a friend like you.

❀

When you decide to do drag, you face many people that disagree with the idea of the art. Drag is a form of self-expression, and it keeps us sane in an ill-minded world. You have to be able to know what is most important to you, and realize that if someone truly cares about you, they will accept anything in the world that gives you your happiness.

❀

I think that it is important to surround yourself with accepting people. If you actually have "friends" that think you are foolish for doing drag, perhaps they should not be your friends. My approach, especially these days, is that of a professional one. If people know you are doing it for money and to entertain people, that can help them decipher the difference between it being a Gig and a sexual proclivity.

❀

Drag for me has always been a personal journey, I do not care what others think as long as I am enjoying the journey. Friends, coworkers, and acquaintances have never given me a hard time; my family cannot get over their own personal shit with me doing drag.

❀

I believe I am doing what was meant for me to do in life. If you do not support that or give constructive criticism than I do not need the negativity

❀

I get past it. I do as I see fit for myself! Live your life for you, do as you chose! No one's opinion should deter you from what you desire; good bad or indifferent. Make yourself happy and everything else will fall into place!

❀

You have to have proper communication, the issue with today is simply people do not committee to the standards of drag, the place stuff on, a wig and call it a day. I follow guidelines and choose to talk and reason, find out why and what is wrong to get proper feedback instead of bashing.

❀

I learned early in the game you need tough skin to make it. Make sure you have a core group that you can go to when times get tough and they are there to fully support and back you. Those core friends will be your support and can and will get you through anything.

❀

When I was doing drag, I stayed true to myself. Things have changed through the years. To make it as a drag impersonator or impersonator, you need to change also. I also learned a lot from the people before and took them advice to heart. I won two titles as a drag king.

❀

I know when I get onstage it is something I love to do and enjoy it. There are going to be haters out there who will try to shoot you down with cruel and mean things. Remember to keep being you and continue moving forward never look back because there are ones that adore and love you for who you are what you are. Keep your chin up and never look down.

❀

I just do what makes me happy. If they are trying to tear you down because you do drag, then they are not much of a friend. Friends stand behind you on your choices of profession, not tear you down.

❀

Self-confidence is very important in drag. There is always someone else around the corner. You just do your thing that makes you happy and do not worry about what others think. All that matters, is drag makes you happy. Try to connect with somebody that has the same interest as you another entertainer that similar that maybe you can pair up and work with.

❁

Do not discount a friend's advice just because it may hurt your feelings. Remember, sometimes it takes a true friend to give you the bad news along with the good. Sit down with them; bring them into your goals. True friends help you achieve success. Ask yourself also, "what have I done to help this friend achieve their dreams too?"

❁

I get past being knocked down by never having a quitter's attitude. Every time someone tells me I cannot do something, I do it to the best of my ability and never give up

❁

I do not do drag for my friends, although their support is amazing. I do drag because I enjoy entertaining a crowd. There will always be things I can do to better myself as an entertainer. I am sure that goes for everyone; no one is perfect. Do it for yourself, in order to succeed in drag; then you can do it to entertain. You should never do it just for the approval of your friends.

❁

At the end of the day, I look at everyone and laugh. It takes a lot of courage and strength to go on any stage and be an entertainer. I personally recommend when you practice, look in the mirror, and tell yourself no matter the outcome of the show "I have and will give it my all." Win or lose, I must leave my best performance on that stage and will continue to push myself to do better.

❁

I had very supportive friends in the beginning, though then they did not seem to take my drag performances very seriously as I did. So eventually, they came less and less to my shows and it did hurt a little but it did not stop me from being a performer.

❁

I explain why I do drag and people usually understand and actually embrace me. I believe people will embrace you if you find confidence on and offstage. For me drag is an art form where I get to express my acting side without committing to a theatre group (that I do not have time for). It is extremely important to practice, practice, practice… Practice your lip-syncing in the mirror. Practice your makeup. Find someone who will teach you the little things like pads and hair. I have made many mistakes but it is from those mistakes that you learn what not to do.

❁

I get past this by reminding them that this is my life to live as I chose. I tell them if they cannot support me then I cannot have them in my life. I have spent so much of my life depressed because I am not what people want me to be. I have accepted the fact that I do not need any person's blessing to be who I am, but my own. As for the friends who say I am no good at drag, I remind them that drag is what you make it. My vision of myself is just that, my vision.

❀

Someone who knocks down what you love and are passionate about is not a friend. Sometimes the hardest thing is to let go of the people have been so close to you because they end up being someone negative in your life. Surround yourself in positivity.

❀

Those are not friends. The moment I find out I am not supported or I am being talked down upon, I distant myself from those people. You have to draw the line for which friends are positive and which friends are negative.

❀

My friends were terrible. They called me a "booger." You know, "booger," as in snot from your nose. I thought I had lost them three weeks before Christmas. It was not until Christmas Eve when I started unwrapping presents from them, that I realized they were going to be friends for the long haul. Here we were living in Kansas, far from any drag impersonators to call a friend, and in my stocking were books. My six friends bought me books on makeup, half dozen of them from the Todd guy creating this book, and several books by RuPaul. They still thought I was a booger, but they loved me so much, that the thought of me being hurt, empowered them to help me find my path.

❀

If performing is what makes you happy, then that is really all that matters. To rise above all those who have an opinion on whether my drag is "good" or not, I am continuously striving to be better, to up my game, to push the envelope, and to prove that I can learn and grow as an entertainer.

❀

I smile and say "To each their own." I turn their negativity into a positive and get busy making sure I am doing my best and give my all with every performance. I use it to motivate me.

❀

All of pre-drag friends love that I am doing it and are my largest fan base.

❀

They are not my friends if they are knocking me down. To address those that do in the most professional way, I ignore them and continue to do as best I can to project a positive, meaningful message as a king, performer, advocator, and supporter.

❀

I work harder to teach myself new skills.

❀

My drag mother used to knock me down so she could make herself feel better. She was afraid to take chances but I was not. I looked in my heart to see what I wanted to do… and I did it. What she said/did no longer mattered after that.

❀

It hurts when you people say you are not good enough. My feelings were hurt when friends said I am too fat to be doing that person or my makeup needed great improvement before I even stepped on that stage to impersonate anyone. My advice is to believe in yourself, do not listen to what other friends or impersonators say. Sometimes they are just jealous because they know you will become a great performer and outshine them.

❀

I think you should first consider is drag really something you love to do and want to make a career out of (or some other sort of long-term commitment). Is it something you feel you can be successful at and enjoy? Drag is NOT for everyone, it is a lot of fun, but many difficulties come along with it. Your friends may be seeing something from their perspective that you cannot (or would not) see. If you feel drag is a true calling for you, then you may want to re-examine these relationships. Friends should be supportive of your hopes and dreams as long as you are not hurting yourself or others. It can be hard to let people go from our lives, but sometimes you need to in order to find your truly valuable friends.

❀

Friends do not knock me down but they do base state their opinion on what I should or should not do. Your "real, true friends" will support you no matter what. If they knock you down… get new friends.

❀

I went out and got to know the performers and who respected them and who did not. I got to know them and became friends with many of the big names of today. I limited my time in bars and clubs so that I would not get a worn out reputation of being a daily drag dresser. I only went out in drag when I was perfection or going to a performance. Immediately after the show, I would say my goodbyes and leave. No one likes a drunken drag impersonator. You will make one or two good friends and have many acquaintances. Pick whom you tell your private business to and leave drama at home.

❈

Only I can determine who is a friend. It takes both parties to keep a friendship. Never be so insecure that you believe "someone destroying or diminishing your value," is a friend.

❈

Be true to yourself and what you feel is your true creative self as well. Not everyone is going to embrace what you do and that is okay. No two entertainers are alike, and not every audience will appreciate what you bring. Grow a thick skin and deal best you can. If there are other entertainers to reach out to, do not be afraid to do so. I encouraged a newbie to reach out to someone well respected in our community that she was terrified to speak to, much less ask for help. When I finally got her passed the point of fear, she reached out with a little help. Now she is a well-respected impersonator and a family member of the terrifying impersonator's house. Never underestimate yourself or those around you.

❈

I try not to take in negative comments towards me when I do drag. I believe I am good at it because I am myself and I try not to let people judge me because I am different and I choose to do drag. I do not let people negativity define me as a person or me performing it is what I enjoying doing.

❈

The very first time I did drag, I was seventeen for a Halloween contest. At first, my friends liked it because they thought it was all fun and games. A couple of them decided that it was not fun anymore when I started to do it for a living. They told me many times that I am too tall for a drag, that I am not drag enough, and many other reasons. The truth is, if you are happy with yourself and what you are doing in life and your friends do not accept you for who you are then they are not really your friends. A true friend would accept you NO MATTER WHAT. If they do not pay your rent, your car, or your bills then do not pay them no mind.

❈

Before you are offended, look deep within, and ask yourself if their comments are coming from a critical place or are they critiquing you? Take the information; digest it to see what areas can be improved on. If it is from a critical place, thank the person and remove oneself from the situation. Responding will only add to escalation.

❈

I have been involved in the Arts in some way since I was four years old. I have been in drag since the night I turned eighteen. Folks, I have told me, "I am not <insert adjective here> enough." My inward response is, "Bitch, please. If I am as piss-poor as you say I am, why then have I won three pageants?"

❈

BE PREPARED. This is a rough industry. Someone will always have a comment, advice, or what they consider you would be good at. Develop a tough skin, let negativity roll off your back, and remember IF IT MAKES YOU HAPPY then that is all that matters!

❀

I was very fortunate. My friends were very supportive when I started to do "Male Drag" I firmly believe that if they cannot be supportive and feel the need to knock you down, then they are not true friends to begin with.

❀

It all depends on your own interpretation of your art. In the beginning, there is a lot of needed improvement. However, you have to be very wary of whose advice you take. You could be adopted by a seasoned Drag impersonator to whom see's something in you, takes you under her wing, and further refers you as her daughter.

❀

I tell myself that if I am happy doing what I do, then my true friends will want to see me do what makes me happiest. The others are not true friends.

❀

I generally do not allow negative influences in my personal life and most people know I do drag. Drag peers have told me that I am "not afraid to be ugly." In some contexts and possibly in its original interpretation, this could have been a cutting form of slander, but I took it as a compliment. In a world of pretty, polished, professionals, there does not seem to be enough experimentation / interpretation. This is my niche and those that understand it applaud what I do.

❀

Some believe I am too old. When I am told I should not do drag, I try harder to prove them wrong.

❀

My gayz always thought for some reason I was cheating when it came to altering my body to compete and perform. I was ALWAYS feminine and had feminine features, but once you see the transgender girls competing in pageants, I strived to be like them. I actually put my award-winning talent on hold sometimes because not many had both talent and beauty! I was determined. Looking back, I probably would not have gone as far with silicone injections for its proven to be deadly. I urge the up and coming impersonators to stick with your talent and the beauty will eventually shine through!

❀

My friends have been very supportive outside of drag. Usually my "friends" in the drag community tend to be harsh. They are just trying to keep the art form of drag as polished as possible. You as an individual have to figure that out how to turn a negative comment into a positive one.

❀

Believing in yourself and not giving into the negativity of others really has to be a drag impersonators' primary mantra. This frame of mind is not always easy to maintain as we as entertainers are evaluated on a daily basis by peers, colleagues, and the general public on social media. Confidence starts from within. For instance as a young entertainer I was "mean-girled" by some of the local impersonators in my hometown. Their unkind words and gestures taught me valuable lessons, to treat others as you would like be treated. I did not like how that felt and I vowed never to make anyone else feel that way. All the lessons one learns on their journey contributes to their wisdom and confidence. It takes time to realize fully ones' self. Criticism from others is unavoidable, but can be applied productively to build your confidence and survival skills.

❁❁

"Housing in America is not permanent.
Even a mighty oak can be transplanted."
Todd Kachinski Kottmeier

Chapter Two

❀❀❀

Many people do not tell their neighbors of their drag identity, and feel unsafe or scared. Discuss your advice on finding a positive path.

Note: To maintain the integrity of this project, I did not edit most of the postings to allow the message sent in, to be in the actual words of the impersonator. I left them anonymous to allow the reader to understand them without pre-conceived bias.

❀

Lordy, lordy, lordy. You must have met my neighbor. I tried hard not to leave my home in drag, but on those late nights, after the bar is closed, my feet begin screaming for mercy. All I can think of is my pillows… the only clear path is to rush home fully dressed (except for perhaps now my heels are replaced by sneakers), to shower and hit the bed. Eventually someone in the neighborhood will figure it out. The secret becomes harder when you live in an active neighborhood near the places you perform, or you become more popular in the community. As I said, eventually the cat is out of the bag. I will not pretend that the neighbors were thrilled. There were no selfie moments with them; they did not bake me cookies. They did not sit in front of my house on Christmas singling "Deck the Halls." Instead, they tossed fruit over the fence into my backyard and shouted derogatory comments. Well, "fuck them." I installed a camera, caught their behavior on tape, and confronted them. "Either you stop all this shit or I share this video with the police department." Needless to say, they moved. On a lighter note though, my other neighbor, this wonderfully older women thought my drag persona is my girlfriend. Perhaps she is, perhaps she is…

❀

This is a hard solution. Believe me, when I was young, you were placing your life on the line in most cities and towns by walking outside cross-dressing. What you think was fun, others considered a threat. Times are changing, but there are still ugly people willing to hurt and kill out of fears far greater than the subject of this book. Never believe you are stronger than their fear. Something I learned in the army, and I am a big and strong guy… even the strongest and biggest guy can be brought down by a single bullet. Be careful. Do not read one of the posts in this section shouting, "Ignore them, it's your life." Try not to encourage violent people to harm you. You are not making a statement in your community if you are in the hospital because four ignorant assholes beat you up with baseball bats. We all have friends that were hurt; a few of us have dead friends. Do not let yourself be the next story in another book. If someone finds out and you live in a place to be feared, take precautions. Carry that mace, install those cameras near your home, park in lighted areas, travel at night with friends, document in your home unusual incidents, tell friends, create a log or diary. We are getting close to acceptance, but close is not the destination... it is only the direction.

❀

Of course there is always a neighbor or friend that finds out and may turn their back or walk the other direction. Not everyone is going to be a fan and that is okay. Just continue to be you and be proud of that. You never know whose eye you will catch or head will turn in support of what you do.

❀

Find what makes you feel safe. Guard dog, security system, etc.

❀

Be yourself be open and honest. Carry yourself with pride and confidence. Be open to questions and even criticizing. It is surprising how many people today are accepting and supportive. Many will stand by you if you are not ashamed of what you do. Change your thoughts to change your outcome.

❀

If someone is outed and their neighbors have a problem, then you know what? Oh well!! Everyone has opinions and what people "think" of you is none of your business. You do you and only the ones that matter will be by your side at the end of the day.

❀

In this life still you always have to be extra cautious

❀

That is always an awkward question when you tell them you are a performer.... "Wait you are a stripper?" I tend to focus on choreography not as just a male impersonator.

❀

Be yourself. Teach them by explaining your craft.

❀

If you are outed then there is no going back in the closet. Though feelings of fear and uncertainty are normal, try to remain positive. Thanks to RuPaul's Drag Race, drag is becoming more mainstream. People are more interested in drag now because of this. You also never know, one of your neighbors could be a former performer with knowledge to share.

❀

I currently live in a very small town, and 99% of population is families man/wife, so being gay in this small town I look onto my neighbors for help as in promoting what I like to do is drag doing benefits and fundraisers for my community.

❀

Random act of kindness. If you have concerns about your neighbors understanding of you, then help them understand you. Give a random act of kindness whenever possible so they do not see you as some mysterious monster with some unsavory nightlife engagements. Show them your humanity. Be neighborly… bring someone a pie. It still actually works (or offer beer). The power of the pastry is strong. Be smart and be safe about it, if you are worried about some burly redneck, do not get too close and no sudden movements. Really though, bring a friend with you if you need to.

❀

Continue with your life as best as possible as it was before you were outed. Sometimes we think up scenarios worse than reality. If people ask questions and you are comfortable, use it as an educational opportunity. If you are not tell them where they can find more info.

❀

Never find yourself alone. We come home from the bar late and I know sometimes alone, one thing I suggest might be not coming or going from your house in drag to avoid making things more complicated.

❀

For me this is a hobby. So when discussed I frame it as my alternative to drinking, drugs, hunting, fishing, golf, etc…

❀

I have not experienced hate from neighbors from doing drag, but I would recommend anyone who feels unsafe to create a collective group of friends nearby that you can go to when feeling unsafe or scared.

❀

People think there is a rule that they have to tell everyone what they do. You do not. If you know you would not be okay, do not do it. There is no shame in keeping the things that bring you pleasure to yourself. If you are outed, it is hard, but people get over it. Find a support system that knows you and can help you when things get scary. Do not be afraid of seeking help from people who have gone through the same. They will know better than anyone on how to get through it.

❀

I am very open about my drag career. There is nothing to be ashamed of.

❀

Telling people that you are a drag impersonator is almost like coming out all over again. The few neighbors that I do talk to know that it is what I do. To me, the makeup, the clothing, and the attitude are your armor. I have never felt unsafe in my neighborhood, which again, I feel very lucky. You just have to own it. There are always going to be negative people in the world. If you are dealing with people like that, invite them to your next show. Show them what you do and how badass you are. Listen to Blow Me (One Last Kiss) by P!nk.

❀

Many times I needed a battery jumped before I finally bought a brand new car. I was very confident. I would make it a ritual to go next door, on both sides of my home to make nice. They would jump my car and some of the boys wanted to jump my bones. I have lived in my own home in Clearwater Florida for twenty-five years. This doll was not careless with her coins! The neighbors were always kind and open-minded. To the left of my home is an elderly couple who always had hot family members over, and was more than happy to watch my house while I doing the pageant circuit. I was gone as Miss Gay USofA and promoting me becoming Miss Continental for two full years. To my right of my home was a younger generation couple who moved in after the original owner passed away. Her name was Noel (same as my mother). Noel would look out for me, but the new owners not so much, but they sure did enjoy "the pot." They thought I was some hot chick off to the strip club and were more than happy giving me a jump. Confidence and charm always got me far. In front of my house was a huge white Baptist Church. I am a non-practicing Catholic, but I thought, "I am surrounded by love." I am safe. Now the church has turned into a Narcanon Center for drug rehabilitation, drug education, and drug prevention programs. Go figure!

❀

I would try to muster my courage and push on because everyone deserves to go about their lives.

❀

I try to be as open and honest as I can. I put everything about myself out there right when I meet someone. "I am a pansexual Transgender man who is also a drag king"; it allows people to know me right away. Then if they have a problem with that I go from there. There is not really any surprises when you get to know me.

❀

When I do not feel safe in my area I always make sure I have someone there. There is safety in numbers.

❀

I was private about it but eventually when I told my neighbors they were pretty cool with it. It is a changing world where we are all learning acceptance for one another. Sometimes we have a turtle in a pack of rabbits but that's okay, the turtle will catch up.

❀

As an impersonator, I take pride in my passion. I do not hide it because it is who I am. Anything that gives me joy in my life should not be hidden from the world. I would suggest that you learn how to accept it as who you are through time by spreading the word of what an impersonator or entertainer truly is.

❀

Tell the neighbor's wife or husband that their spouse is cheating on them! I am joking. Again, make sure they are clear it is not a sexual thing and its entertainment. Invite them to a show. If they are making you feel unsafe, call the authorities or get other neighbors who approve of your life to back you up and talk some sense into them. Perhaps, simply ignore them as best you can.

❀

Drag for me has always been activism so the more visible the better. I hold my head high because I can see the work I am doing is creating safe places for all in my small town. I was very fearful at first to let anyone in my town know. I was very surprised; for the most part everyone was understanding and even supportive

❀

I would feel the neighborhood out to make sure it is compatible with my lifestyle

❀

Everyone deserves privacy in their own home. No one should have to hide if it is you. If it gets bad, perhaps you should move, get a dog, or buy a gun!

❀

Sometimes being afraid is too much. Accept who you are with pride. Fear simply shows you are afraid to be you. So smile, move on, and get past it. They could support you. If not, get a restraining order. <enter smile here.>

❀

I would keep others updated if you feel unsafe. Let trusted people know when you are leaving and when you should arrive, so someone has your back in case of an emergency.

❀

I found in helps to be honest about who I am and what I do. Do not let anyone make you feel scared or unsafe. Hold your head high to show them you are not scared. This is just their way to bully you.

❀

Being outed is not good at all. If you are feeling unsafe and scared, reach out to the people that love and accepts all of you; you are not alone.

❀

You should never feel unsafe or scared because you do drag. If it is a bad neighborhood, maybe think of moving. I also carry a gun.

❀

When I started out I was an undercover police officer. That was in the seventies when female impersonation was not accepted, as it is today. Now all of my neighbors know. They come to my shows and they look forward to seeing me; sometimes I stop by before I leave. Everybody comes around eventually, as long as they are educated and understand. If you have been outed by one of your neighbors, they may not approve and try to rub it in your face. Just go on about your own business and life. If you feel intimidated by a certain neighbor maybe there is a way to have a communication and make them understand that it is part of your personality.

Speak to them. Ask them what they do and show general interest in their life too. Maybe there is an underline reason. Always have an open mind and be respectful.

❊

Stay confident in being yourself. If you are scared that people cannot accept you, stay around positive people. It will help you feel loved and safe.

❊

Let your neighbors find trust and love in you out of drag first. The conversation of illusion will come up as you get to know each other. If you do not feel safe with your neighbors, I suggest remaining low key. The option to get ready at a bar or club is always there so you can keep that side of you private.

❊

Be even more open, invite them to a show, let them see your drag room full of costumes. By putting their fears at ease, you also ease your own.

❊

I am fortunate enough to live in a neighborhood that is pretty gay-friendly. I live in a building with many entertainers residing in it. My advice would be to keep your head up, stand confident, and be smart about your surroundings.

❊

Get to know your neighbors. That is the best way to break through any misconceptions they have regarding drag and entertainers. If you see them outside when you are in face, always make sure you say, "Hi." Make light of it and make them laugh. Laughter is always the best icebreaker.

❊

I live in downtown San Diego, outside the safety of the Gayborhood of Hillcrest. At first, I was scared of walking in face from my apartment over to my parking structure across Broadway. I would nearly run, dragging my drag suitcase behind me. When I first started, it took me about four hours to apply my makeup, so getting ready at a venue was not really an option. I finally figured, who cares? With as many crazy things as you can see walking around today, a man walking down the street wearing boy clothes and a beautiful face really is not that bad.

❊

Finding a positive path means to have a positive attitude, image, and aura about oneself. This will become even stronger when the neighbors are not being nosy and question the late night departures or entering.

❊

I ask myself if the people in my neighborhood really matter. They do not pay my expenses, and I am sure that there are aspects of their loves that I would not find overly appealing. I think that this puts us on even ground.

❊

I am fortunate enough to have completely understanding neighbors.

Unless you are in jail and cannot determine your neighborhood... pick your surroundings. I was forced to move for my own protection. If I do not protect myself, than there is no drag. "Me" without a drag face must always come first. Being harmed by an idiot, or my home being vandalized and memories destroyed, does not make me a stronger impersonator. Nobody is asking me to be a marty.

❀

It is hard to give advice about this question. My neighbors use to be really good friends of mine until they found out. They had all neighbors sign a letter to have me move. When I moved into the new neighborhood, they knew we were gay. When they found out I did drag, I was hated and called a child molester. After a few months, some of the ladies would come over to see if I could help them with makeup or to do hair. Now as for the men, well I was always asked for sex.

❀

Safety in drag should always be your first consideration. Are you able to get ready with friends at home? Better yet, can you get ready at a friend's house located in a safer location or the venue where you are performing/working? How well do you know your neighbors? Have you had an honest, sober conversation with your neighbors about your drag and that you are not actually an evil baby-sacrificing devil worshipper? I mean look, your job and/or creative expression is nobody's damn business; but if you are trying to maintain good relations with your neighbors try to talk to them. Most people are reasonable and cannot hate people if they know them. Have a friendly conversation in a public place for safety reasons. At the end of the day if you are threatened by someone or are unsafe, call the police. Your safety should be your number one concern. Do not let an unsafe situation spin out of control.

❀

I just would not throw it in their face. Do not leave your house in full drag unless your neighbors are very cool with it.

❀

If your neighbors are good people, they will understand that you are an entertainer. Have self-respect at all times. Do not act like drag trash or you will never get anyone's respect.

❀

I have never bothered about such things. I do not invade my neighbor's privacy and they act the same. I am sure; however, they have seen the rather statuesque redhead that leaves the house from time to time. Never approached from the new neighbors, but my next door knows. She has seen pictures, my DVD, and she knows my partner and me intimately.

❀

My neighbors found out by happenstance. They were coming home from a straight bar and me from the gay bar. They did not recognize me at first. The next day was different. I explained and invited them to a show. Then we became friends.

A friend of mine did not have the same luck. I suggested she remove at least her drag face when returning home from a show. Do not flaunt it or deny your true self, but take care not to provoke ignorance into action.

❀

It is out of the norm I guess to let your neighbors know. It is your choice. It was hard for me to overcome at first because people are mean and rude. They kept telling me that I wanted to be a man. I love being a women, dressing up as a men. Dancing is fun and it is who I am. Be conformable with yourself and people will take it or leave it.

❀

With my neighbors, it is a mix. I have neighbors on one side who just hate my wife and me because we are part of the LGBTQ community in general. Our neighbors across the street have been very friendly. When they found out about me performing, I was walking out of my garage to my car in face to head to a show. The questions started then, but I had to leave so I said I would talk to them about it the following day. The next day I explained all about drag kings/male impersonators. They were very interested. I have invited them to shows but most have young children.

❀

The best way to address this situation may be to actually go talk to the person face to face and explain what drag. If they are still hesitant, let them know you would like to live in a peaceful manner and get along in the best possible way. If the person seems threatening, remove yourself from the situation and avoid this person if possible.

❀

When I first started out, I would only (and I stress "only") dress and paint at the venue itself and reverse the process prior to going home for the night. As time went on, I began to adopt a "Fuck 'em and feed 'em Skittles" mentality. That is not to say I have not been gay bashed. You can believe I have, but I live as a girl because I am "a girl."

❀

I am not necessarily one to care about what other's think about me or what I do. I have enough supporters not to have to think twice about the ones who have a problem with it. They are not living with me or paying my bills, so why worry about it?

❀

I have not had an issue living in Austin, Fort Lauderdale, or Poughkeepsie, New York. Sometimes, it is all in how you handle yourself. There are those that may talk or snicker behind your back or to your face. I always represented myself as an entertainer and invited people to the show if they see me on the way out. An invitation sometimes goes a long way.

❀

My neighbors know I perform, however, I do arrange for someone to drive me home from the venue, usually an employee if it is an option. They wait until I go inside my home before driving away.

❀

Part of the path to being a seasoned performer is developing the confidence to face adversity. Many people try drag during Halloween or a talent contest. They discover it is not their passion. Many of what appeals to the audience is not the look, the style, or the music, but the inspiration that you bring either being your authentic self or your character and your belief in its longevity. Use that strength and passion to redefine misconceptions of the neighbors. Years ago, people used to say that they did not know any gay people. That has now changed. Now they will be able to say they know an impersonator too. Be the new trend.

❀

I believe honesty and respect with other people is important. I always try to be up front about who I am wherever I go. I learn who is comfortable and who may not be. I act accordingly to each person I encounter.

❀❀

> "Do you notice the people with the most insecurities are the same people belittling others? Strength is not built on backs of the fallen."
> Todd Kachinski Kottmeier

Chapter Three

❀❀❀

For many impersonators, the ugliest words shared are not by the haters, but by other entertainers. Few of those performers creating such negative words will see themselves in this question. This is not to address the hater, but the impersonator struggling to look past the words. Help them.

Publisher's Note: We sent out thousands of invitations to participate in this project. Almost every single one ignored me. Most of the performers refused to pass on the invitation to their peers. When contacted, they told me, "Todd, being hard on the performers gives them thick skin. It thins out the weak people and advances the craft. Obviously, the entertainers participating in this book... disagreed with them.

Note: To maintain the integrity of this project, I did not edit most of the postings to allow the message sent in, to be in the actual words of the impersonator. I left them anonymous to allow the reader to understand them without pre-conceived bias.

❀

Please! You will look back at this one day, and shake your head and laugh. I often sit here at my vanity in the dressing room, as if looking back upon my life, reflecting at the incredible moments leading up to where I am now. I do not think of the haters, the people that looked down upon me, and told me I would never make it. They were wrong. I proved it over and over again. My drag room bursts with memories they will never understand. I have mentored, hosted, taught, and inspired more people than they ever will in their lives. I became one of the creators of this craft because, unlike them, I believed in the best of people. I understood, "to make this craft advance, we all had to become better together." We all had to become leaders. I love where I am in life. It was a journey built of love and admiration. I often wonder about those other people that lived life so jaded and filled with anger... if they ever stopped and realized they stole and sacrificed their own cherished memories.

❀

I hate hearing impersonators tearing each other down. I think of some of the greatest singers in my life growing up: Karen Carpenter, Cher, Carly Simon, Ella Fitzgerald, and even Barbra Streisand. Each admit to being shy and reserved, almost to a crushing level in their early years. I doubt they all became stars because they survived bullying. They blossomed because someone held their hands and helped them past their insecurities. If a peer is bullying you, it is "on them." People can be beautiful and talented and still be a pig. How many times have you in life heard someone say, "This person is so pretty on the outside but their heart is so ugly?" Ignore ugly hearted performers that believe "getting to the top means trampling over others." You will never get them to understand, but I will tell you one thing, "if you do not step in when someone else is being beat down, than your apathetic behavior makes you just as bad as the bully!"

❀

I have been called a booger, fat, ugly, and not talented. You have to be comfortable in your own skin and portray the best possible you that you can be. Often, those that lash out do so because of a "jealous factor" perhaps in which they forget that you are all in the same arena. Maybe not on the same platform, but generally speaking, we all hold the same position. Perhaps you are not good enough from them, but you are great to others. It is their opinion, and opinions.

❀

Misery loves company, stay surrounded by those who love you and care for you. Leave the haters to be miserable alone.

❀

Your mirror will never lie to you. Look at what is said, while considering whom it is coming from. Never allow someone else's opinion or words dictate who you are. Know and embrace your flaws; relish in what is good.

❀

People are going to talk no matter whom you are, whether you are a great impersonator or a horrible one. Concentrate on you and only you.

❀

If you are told your make-up needs work, ask them to show you. If they say you have crappy costumes, ask them to help. If they say you have no stage presence, ask them to be specific. If you cannot ask anybody, search for it on the internet. If you really want to do better, there are many ways to learn the craft. Show them you took their "constructive" criticism and put it to good use to out-shine them!

❀

The ugliest and most viscous words can often come from your peers and coworkers. Remember one thing, negativity always stems from fear. The people that run their mouths the most are usually threatened in some manner. It is a reaction and really is their problem. Why waste your valuable time trying to figure them out?

❀

As a drag impersonator who has had to deal with shade, my best advice is to remember that they are not you. Your drag is your drag. Any other entertainer who says something ugly is just jealous.

❀

As long as other entertainers are talking about you, then keep up the good work. You are doing something right!

❀

This happens more often than it should in our community. It has happened to me more times than I can count. Be true to yourself. Trying to fit into the mold others want you to be in, will not make you happy, and generally will not make you a better performer. Be proud of who you are and hold your head high.

❀

This is a hot topic, no matter your city. If you begin being successful with your talent, and others begin making plans at being at your shows vs someone else's show... drama will strike. Gay, straight, trans*, if someone can dream of a bashing for you, that may defer your audience to go elsewhere, it will happen. Honestly, the best thing to do, is not get caught up in it. Act as if you have no clue, because chances are they are talentless. If they go to watch another show, do not get offended, you do not own your audience. The quickest way to lose your audience, is going on social media, to talk about beating someone down with a bottle. No one wants to be a part of drama. They do not care about and you will lose their interest. If you have talent and you truly only want the best for your community, your audience will see it and they will be there supporting you all the way.

❀

Most cases, they are just jealous.

❀

It is always best to avoid the inevitable drama and gossip of the drag scene. My approach has always been to act as if drag is another job and conduct myself with class, professionalism, and reliability. That means staying away from any negative nonsense. If it means booking other shows because one attracts the wrong element, so be it. Rise above!

❀

Remember, we all started somewhere. No one started out "sickening" or "gorgeous" right away. Every single performer has made mistakes onstage. Like Jynxx Monsoon said, "Water off a ducks back*." Keep with it and before you know it you will be a seasoned performer as well. For every one performer that made a negative comment there will be two with a good one. Surround yourself around the positive performers and not the negative ones. Though it may be tempting, is best not to lash out at them. Just smile and go about your craft.

* Actual cited quote, "That's my gift. I let that negativity roll off me like water off a duck's back." George Foreman

❀

Always look in the mirror before going onstage and tell yourself no matter what you are fabulous!

❀

Drag is not about fitting into the box other people believe you belong in, it is about the opposite. Entertainers that do not understand it, does not get drag, so there is really no reason to listen to them. Sometimes you just have to suck it up and let it go. It may sound harsh, but these people are not worth your time. Seek positive influences who are willing to contribute to your growth even if you do not want to hear their constructive criticism. Do not waste your time with people who are going to be destructive. Sharpen your wit by tossing friendly fire back and forth with your friends and helping each other grow a thick skin and a list of witty comebacks for your arsenal. Often to survive in this world, you have to learn to take and dish it. Know which comments to take to heart and who's to take with a grain of salt. Not everyone matters, and not everyone deserves your attention.

❀

My gut reaction answer to this question is just to dismiss whatever they are saying but sometimes, negative comments offer hidden tips. If they make negative comments on your makeup, study your make up. Ask a seasoned impersonator you trust for advice. Take time to work and improve on your makeup skills. Many negative comments empower you to improve upon your craft. There are also times that performers say things just to be mean and hurtful. You have to develop a thick skin quickly and learn to move past it.

❀

Most of the time I have found when people put you down it is because of jealousy or their own lacking in their self-worth. It is a reflection of them, not you. Ignore them or call them on it but do not take it to heart.

❀

I have been bullied by other entertainers. It inspired me to work harder. The song from Neon Trees inspires me the most. "Everybody talks, Everybody talks, Everybody talks too much."

❀

Their words are nothing more than a reflection of their own insecurities. Ignore their crap. Tear da house and show them that you are above them.

❀

The ladies are shady! Do not take them too seriously. People are going to nitpick and find anything they can to drag (no pun intended) you down. Some people do not like a fierce competition. Just do you. Remember, even the prettiest impersonator started as a booger. Practice makes perfect, and remember that when you snatch their crowns.

❀

In the world of drag, you must always be confident of you who you are and of your drag style; this way these type of people will not bother you.

When I first started, I did get some comments about my beard, padding, and that my makeup was not great. To me, my drag persona was every woman. She can be whomever she wants to be. I will say it again. Own what you do. It is an art form, and with art you grow and you change. If other performers are nasty to you, you just have to do "you." Go onstage and give it your all. That is all you can do. If people have negative comments and not constructive ones, they are not your friends. Next! ~Also, listen to "Stupid Girls" by P!nk.

Drag is so subjective, and at the end of the day everyone is not going to like what you bring to the table. What is important is to be true to who you want to be as an entertainer. Over time, you will gain discernment as to individuals who are truly "haters" and those who simply want to help. That is more important than worrying about every comment. At the end of the day, you only should worry about hitting the stage and being better than the last time. Progression is definitely important.

I know you are trying to help people by expressing your experience. You cannot help by passively aggressively posting on social media or never reaching out. People look up to you and you should be showing an example of how you would like to be treated. We need strong secure leaders, not someone with a bad attitude.

I have heard so much drama, backstabbing, and hate within my own community, from "friends," even members of my own drag family. I am a very sensitive person and tend to take on a lot of guilt, blame, shame, and rage when I hear these things. Ultimately knowing who I am and being the best entertainer I can be has helped me rise above all the hate. Nothing is more painful than hearing those ugly words out of people you have loved, trusted, nurtured, and helped. You will not die from words; they may sting but your wounds will heal and help thicken your skin.

Most people who tear you down are usually very insecure.

There is no "right way" to do drag, everyone's style and strengths are different. While advice, feedback, and critiques from other entertainers can help even the most experienced entertainer improve their craft, words meant only to tear down and degrade have no place in the drag community. Find a community that lifts you up and supports your unique style of performance. Seek out ways to improve yourself, the people that are willing to help, and the ones worth keeping around. Find your family, because, at the end of the day, all that matters is having people that love and support you.

To this day, I still have entertainers trashing, reading, and saying hurtful things to me behind my back. I keep reminding myself not to let others stop me from doing what I love. If I had listened to all the negativity thrown at me, I would have stopped doing drag years ago. People say that is part of the business, but it does not have to be if everyone would support each other more instead of tearing each other down. There is a big difference between constructive criticism and critiques; one helps others to grow while the other is just plain mean. For all the negative things being said and done to me, I try to put out twice the positivity for others to show it is about community and love. I would rather be known as an impersonator who helps instead of hurts!

Sometimes you have to stop listening to other entertainers and listen to your audience, the people who come to see you.

While sometimes difficult, always appreciate your own self-worth and the unique experience and talent you bring to the stage. If you are doing less traditional drag, it may be more difficult. Do remember though; you will never be them and they can never be you. Compete with your previous skills to always improve and not spend time on comparisons to others.

When becoming an entertainer you become an image in the LGBT community. How you portray your image is up to you. There will always be "haters" and those fueled by jealousy that will want to crush you. It is your job to rise in a professional manner. We cannot represent a community of love and unity if we fall to the same level of those who want to destroy us. I am hard of hearing but I do not let that stop me from doing what I love. If that cannot stop me, neither can the negative people.

Many times, you will receive cruel words from other impersonators or fellow entertainers that really hurt you. However, you have to pay them no mind because they are struggling with something that you have already succeeded. If anyone has to make you feel poorly about yourself before they feel good about themselves, they are just missing acceptance in their own lives. You have to just breathe and keep on doing you. If it is what you love, you have to be strong minded. Let no one in the industry bring you down.

You need a thick skin to be successful in this industry. Sometimes the harshest of words come from a good place. It is important to take constructive criticism when you know it is genuine.

This can happen in this profession. If you do not have to work with them directly, pay them no mind. If you have to have direct contact with them, remember sometimes you got more flies with honey! Be the nice person. Always go into any situation above reproach. That way if they talk shit about you behind your back, everyone else will wonder why, because you are so nice to everyone. If they are being shady and saying you are bad at drag, evaluate yourself. If you are happy with your drag, keep doing you. If not, get better. Try asking the impersonator who is being a #@and% for her help. Sometimes the best way to turn an enemy into a friend is to befriend them. Tell her you think that some of what she says is valid, and you think she could really help you. Sometimes people are just assholes because of fear. There is nothing you can do; just worry about yourself.

❀

It is a sad fact that some of the worst behavior I have witnessed has been from one performer to another. The best advice I can give is just do what you want because you love it. That is what is great about drag; there are no rules, it is about breaking the rules and bringing an authentic part of yourself out.

❀

Know your self-worth. Be you no matter what!

❀

If performers tell you, "You need to have thick skin to be successful in drag," are they saying "Learning the craft and being taught to be talented, and eventually talent..." are less important than bullying.

❀

The GLBTQ community is our worst critic. Be comfortable in your own skin. People's opinions matter most to themselves. Never be afraid to be you!

❀

To be honest with the person you are because bashing people for who they are is stupid and uncalled for. No one (and I mean no one) is perfect. You have to strive to do greatness and cannot just sit on your ass and buy cheap stuff and expect respect. Work for it, become Coti Collins, Derrick Barry, Cierra Desiree Nichole, Kirby Kolby, Jessica Jade, and Brooke Lynn Heights. You have to smile at those people to realize at that sometimes they are simply helping. Often tough love is too much.

❀

"Sticks and stones will break my bones But words will never harm me." *

---

* "Sticks and Stones" is an English language children's rhyme. It persuades the child victim of name-calling to ignore the taunt, to refrain from physical retaliation, and to remain calm and good-natured. It is reported by Gary Martin. "The Phrase Finder." Retrieved September 22, 2012 to have appeared in The Christian Recorder of March 1862, a publication of the African Methodist Episcopal Church, presented as an "old adage" in this posted form above. The phrase was updated when it again appeared in 1872, as advice in Tappy's Chicks: and Other Links Between Nature and Human Nature, by Mrs. George Cupeoplees. The version used in that work runs: "Sticks and stones may break my bones, but names will never hurt me."

At the end of the day, you need to remember the old fable "sticks and stones." The only person that can bring you down is you. Remain strong and confident, do you, be you because the second you try to conform is the second you lose your passion in the art form.

❀

I have been around; I have seen and heard many of these kinds of things. I think it is sad that we all cannot get along in the drag world; it is hard enough as it is. I have found that a lot of it is because they are jealous. The more they act out, the better you become. All of the acting out got them nowhere. They are just words; the more they act out, the worse it is on them. No one likes impersonators that treat others with no respect. We are performers and we are out there to entertain.

❀

There are entertainers who will say mean cruel hateful things; some are hard to look past or get over. Remember you are not like the haters, You are you and that is what makes you. Shine like a star and kill them with kindness. Two wrongs do not make a right.

❀

Words are just that, words. Learn from critiques, but do not let words become discouraging. They may have come from nothing and had to work their way up. Do not let hateful words stop you. Keep on trying and learning. One day you will find yourself on the top.

❀

If another entertainer or impersonator offends you, than pull them aside to say, "I do not put you down for your talent or your looks, so I would appreciate it if you did not do it to me." Tell them you respect them for what they do and ask for the same respect. Some people are catty (spiteful, snide). They may try to make it a joke, but you know this is how they feel. Be nice to them. I will give them a guilt-complex. I have never experienced this to my face though they may have said something behind my back.

❀

My peers are the worst. They are either into it fully and dog when they see someone that is not as they are. I am a comedic drag impersonator. I do not shave anything but my face. My partner was starting out in drag. I gave her many positive remarks, but she dogged me constantly about taking drag more seriously. I told her I was not into the pageant impersonator stuff like her. I had to stand up for myself. I know I bring laughter and joy to my audience. Remember, it is not about looking pretty. It is about what you give out. It will returns to you tenfold!

❀

Stay strong; never let negative people knock you down. Always hold your head high. Drama impersonators and impersonators are out to make you doubt and dislike yourself. Never knock yourself down. Remember, you beautiful and amazing

❀

It is hard and hurtful dealing with negativity from other entertainers. Keep your head up. Honestly if they see a reaction from you, they will continue. If you tend to ignore them, they will stop (maybe not right away, but they will stop). Do not stop doing something you enjoy because of other entertainers. Remember why you enjoy drag in the first place. Make friends with entertainers that want to help you and are positive. Sometimes someone else is just jealous and just like in high school when the jealousy is there the bullying occurs. Keep your head up, master your craft, and show them you would not let them scare you from what you enjoy.

❈

They call me out regarding my teeth, I struggled even as a boy. I remind myself, "An ugly soul is far worse than ugly teeth." I have a good strong spirit, and that to me is far more important than my looks.

❈

For me, this has been a constant struggle, not only as a king, but also as a king-sized king. Most entertainers want to do the show for the love of the art form. I say to those who feel they are better than I am in the industry, "if you cannot hire me because I do not fit your requirements or looks, then I will create my own." Never let anyone else make you feel as if you are not good enough. YOU ARE GOOD ENOUGH! Never give up!

❈

When I first started drag sixteen years ago, they criticized me for being different. As a trans-identified performer, it was difficult for some of the other entertainers to understand my performance identity vs. my day-to-day gender identity. They would make hurtful remarks at times and poke fun at me. The stress and anxiety of those situations pushed me toward self-harming thoughts. I decided to make myself a promise to marry the concepts of positive thinking, vulnerability, and integrity. This allowed me to be myself and create art so that others, who also felt ostracized, would have a safe space with me. I did not feed into "drama" or negativity. I found a healthy community and asked to take positions of leadership within them. I have run my own shows for ten years and have kept my drive and integrity intact. Search for kindred spirits and you will find support and inspiration. Always BE TRUE TO YOURSELF.

❈

I do not like hearing performers talk about other performers. We have the confidence to get onstage and display our craft, so why compare or compete with someone else. "Be you." Do not let someone's view of you make you feel like you are less of a performer.

❈

There are veterans of drag embracing or threatened by you and what you bring to the stage. Stay true to yourself. The negative people will either make you strong or quit. If you put your time and dues in, eventually you will be accepted. I find impersonators intimidate and degrade newbies. They are threatened because the new entertainers may get their bookings or become more popular.

There are two types or performers; one will try and help you succeed by giving you constructive criticism, while the others want to be shady and tear another down. You have to figure out which is which. Remember, sometimes people dislike what they cannot understand. Often our art is too abstract for other performers.

Male and female impersonation is what it is, an art form. Nobody does it the same. Keep up the good work and keep practicing to master your craft. Always have someone video your performances, so you see yourself as others do onstage.

Many entertainers rarely last two years because of all the nasty things other entertainers say about to and about them. This is a tough industry. You need very thick skin (and not just for the makeup applied day in and day out) to be able to deal with all the haters you will encounter. You do not perform for other entertainers, but for the fans who love to see you. I do not suggest completely ignoring it. Address it; let them know how you feel. Nine out of ten times, you will mistake a playful read for something sincerely shady.

Other impersonators will definitely put you down. I keep myself distant from the catty people by staying both within my family and those who make me feel good and I belong. You have to smack them to the side and worry about turning it out. Do not let them have control on your future.

I dealt with trash talk from other entertainers for years. The best advice I can give anyone is to keep doing what you are doing. It can be hard to get past the negativity, and those who always seem to want to bring you down, but it IS possible. No matter how many people are talking smack, a select few really know you, and know that you are better than what the haters are spreading. Be better than the haters, do not stoop to their level, and continue being the best person you can be.

I consider the source and intention. To say it does not hurt would be a lie, and I usually cry once alone. When confronted by negative, rude, or mean comments, I will just agree with them saying, "Yes, you are absolutely right." Most times, they are trying to get a negative reaction and by agreeing, most times it stops them in their tracks. I then say something very nice about them and mean it.

The only time negativity bothered me was when it was about something I already felt insecure about, but only when it came from someone admired. It took a longtime to realize those people were actually expressing or projecting their own insecurities onto me. I know the areas I need to grow. If someone negatively points it out to me, I am sure this person has the same issue too. If someone constructively points them out, they have been there too, but they have moved past it. Those are the people you call "sisters." They look out for you, and encourage you to do better.

Everything else is background noise. RuPaul truly stated it best, "Mama said, unless they paying your bills, pay them bitches no mind!" and "What other people think about me is none of my business." Literally, the best advice any impersonator needs to succeed.

❈

Entertainers are sometimes the haters. They have low self-esteem about themselves; they project this onto the positive creator to mark their very soul. Look into that positive soul and nurture it.

❈

People always dislike seeing you better yourself, because it forces them to work harder. Keep being you!

❈

Words are nothing but words; let them say what they will. Do what your heart leads you to do, dig deep and hold your head high. Do not get caught responding to them because that is what they want.

❈

Words told to me included, "You are fat, you are the ugliest impersonator I ever seen, you are a disgrace to the gay world…" I say to them now and to you reading this, "Up there's!" I am someone now and you no longer exist. You claimed to be Miss Big Shot, but now they canceled your show; no one wants you as a performer. As for me, I am still going strong and having a blast doing it. Oh yeah and making them coins hunny!

❈

When fellow entertainers are coming for you with some truly mean-spirited words and thoughts, take a breath and remind yourself why you are doing drag. I hope you are doing drag for yourself because honey, nobody else is going to care if you do not care. Remind yourself that this person is trying to bring you down to their level because of their low self-esteem. Your drag has nothing to do with them. You should be doing this for yourself and no one else; they can either join the party or get the fuck out. More than likely, they are looking for a response from you, so do not give it to them. If it really is a persistent problem, find a way to put a bitch back where she belongs as professionally as possible. Do your best not to burn bridges because you never know who you are going to be required to work with or need a job from in the future, but do not be afraid to defend yourself.

❈

Never let anyone determine your self-worth. Present yourself and your persona to the world as you see fit. Learn from the ones that want to teach. Take what you learn to help finesse your look style and personality as an entertainer.

❈

Accept it with a grain of salt. You must be doing something that threatens their position. Think of it as a good thing. Never acknowledge or speak to others. If someone mentions it, let it go. As long as they are saying my name, I will never be forgotten.

When other entertainers verbally assault "newbies," they forget they were there once newbies too. They should cash their respective reality-checks and recall their past. They need to foster and help the "new blood" coming up. I have found folks that do this are just trying to make themselves feel better by putting others down. "Shake it off" and continue to watch, learn and improve. It takes time to find and master your "look and character." Anything worth having is worth waiting on.

I have learned that the hate from fellow entertainers is most times concern for themselves. "Is he/she is better than me, does he/she perform the same genre of music?" and so on. There are impersonators that do not get why girls dress like boys and girls the same in turn. It is like this, you do not have to understand, but be respectful regardless.

Many of the entertainers and impersonators are haters. They are jealous of what you have to offer or they might be able to fit the crowd a little better. Every entertainer is different and each will have their time to shine or be themselves. People will always hate, but be kind in return. They will not know what to do and you will become the better person.

No one can make a person feel anything that they themselves do not allow. The best way to handle this is to confront them in a civil and peaceful manner. Explain how this makes you feel. If it continues, be careful of what you share with this such said person. Keep everything civil peaceful and at a distance.

I once asked a member of my drag family what the best advice she could give me insofar as drag was concerned. She looked me in the eye and said, deadpan, "Don't." I use that to show where sheer stubbornness pays off.

Try not to associate with those types. Remain classy, avoid drama, and you will have a successful career.

Thankfully, I have never been knocked down. My friends and family have been extremely supportive. I have family members who do not understand the drag lifestyle. They are somewhat taken back by it, but even they have never discouraged me. For those who are, my advice is to follow your passion in spite of what other's may think or say. Drag is an art, another way of self-expression and there is nothing strange or wrong about it. I kid around and tell people, I am paid to suffer from dual personality disorder. <enter grin here.> It's not what other people call you that matters, but what you answer to. Follow your own path, not the path of what others set for you.

Performers will cut you down in the dressing room while you are onstage or anywhere for that matter, except to your face. Usually they are jealous of your talents. When you first begin, you have to figure out what works best for you. No advice is bad advice. Take what helps you and disregard the rest. Even seasoned impersonators have issues with jealousy. This is where you get the thick skin needed in our line of business.

❀

I have always believed that even if I am not the best to take the stage that night, if even one person in the audience enjoyed my performance, then I have done what I was supposed to do. For that reason, I can say I did my best.

❀

Nothing worth doing comes easy. You will have haters in whatever you do and wherever you go. The reason that the comments so negatively affect you is because you do have some level of respect for these people and they are art. Drag is an ever-evolving, ever-changing industry, which requires relearning and reinventing your art. Expect that if the person has viability, that they will eventually learn to accept what you do (but not necessarily you) and make the decision to either gravitate towards or away from your art as a means of education. Many times, you will find them even copying you, which as we say, is the sincerest form of flattery.

❀

Unfortunately, this a reality. When I receive those comments, I tend to always look at the comment and dissect it. Even in negativity, there is positivity. You have to be able to find it.

❀

I will admit when I started I was so young seventeen years old to be exact. Winning Talent shows , working as a show director at The Blue Moon in New Port Richey, other performers were jealous. They did not think I paid my dues. There stemmed hateful name calling and backstabbing. ...sometimes it's the survival of the fittest. ...but if I could rewind I would have killed them with kindness. ...now sometimes my peers and I just tease not with malice but love. It better be!

❀❀

> "If what you have is not enough for
> those around you, change the crowd."
> Todd Kachinski Kottmeier

Chapter Four
❁❁❁

Dating 101
"When do you tell them you are an impersonator?"

Note: To maintain the integrity of this project, I did not edit most of the postings to allow the message sent in, to be in the actual words of the impersonator. I left them anonymous to allow the reader to understand them without pre-conceived bias.

❁

I always laugh at the people that date you because they want to ride my coattail and share my spotlight. I say laugh, but it is not funny. There is nothing funny about someone that dates you because of who you pretend to be... in or out of drag.

❁

You need to consider yourself lucky when a date goes instantly bad because the person expressed their true feelings. How many times do you date someone too long before realizing they are the wrong person for you? Every day, every hour, every moment you spend with the wrong person, is lost "because the person that is looking for you," will not look at you because you are in a relationship. If I focus on myself to become the great person I see in the mirror, then the person I need in my life... will recognize me; will want me for all the right reasons.

❁

This is not a one solution fits all kind of subject. Each person you date will handle you being an impersonator differently, and his or her reactions vary too much to address in a simple comment. Remember, some of the feedback and reactions coming from the person you are dating, may not be coming from them, but how they perceive their friend's will react to dating you.

❁

It is always a gamble. I believe that this is a balancing act as well. Be strong as to who you are and confident; you are a person both in and out of "drag." You can be in a committed relationship as well as to the stage. Balance priorities in order to understand better where the relationship stands, but having an open forum to address the issue in a relationship will better set yourself up for success. If you do receive destructive comments, first, listen. Take a moment to take it in and allow yourself the opportunity to explain yourself, your stance on the relationship as well as the stage career. Allow the opportunity to find a balance between the both of you. It is not something to be forced down someone's throat, but I have found in past as long as you invite them to take part in what you are passionate about, (i.e. back stage, etc.) that they may see the other side of you. Often connecting to other performers' partners will open the door further.

❀

Keep an open mind but watch for" red flags." Listen to your gut feelings; they are usually right. If you find yourself on the negative side of this situation, keep your head up. The right person is still looking for you.

❀

I stress it enough; being open and honest saves you from many pain and embarrassing situations. When things turn serious, explain the situation to them. Allow the person to decide, give them a choice, and respect it but also respect yourselves. If your love for them is stronger than the love for drag, you can give up drag. Never allow bullying or alternatives to dictate your decision.

❀

Just be honest with yourself and the other person. You should not have to hide who you are.

❀

Not everyone can handle the drag spouse role. Right from the beginning, be open and honest about your passion for the craft, BEFORE you emotionally investing in them. They call it, "active listening," to be able to hear exactly what their concerns. Go into the date with the mind-set of, "there is so very much to learn about each other." Take it one-step at a time.

❀

If it is something you really want to do, then you will have to make your decision and be ready for any possible outcome.

❀

"Do not have sex the minute you meet trade!." It sets you up for failure and no return call. All straight men and some gay men have a certain need to be a "Star Fucker!" They just want to experience walking in the room with the DIVA. To them, it is like screwing a "Science Project." Someone once called me these exact words, but only once. I enjoy dinner and a fine wine before they get the goods!

❀

It is as easy as this. You will not ever see me humping someone in the audience, kissing them, or flirting. My partner does not deserve me disrespecting them. The point of performing is just that, to perform and entertain. If you get up there and work your ass off without being slutty onstage, you can still make money. If you are only taking off your clothes, with no dancing or theatrics, consider yourself a glorified stripper.

❀

I never wasted time with people who did not accept it. I dated girls in the past who thought I should not or could not do drag because I am extremely femme. Never let anyone hold you back. I am happy now that I am with someone who not only supports it, but performs with me as well!

❀

Try not to throw yourself into a relationship, though it may be tempting at first. It is okay to be reserved for a little while. This is a good time to turn to your family, drag family, and friends for support. Many negative comments come from a lack of understanding and experience. You never know who's mind you can change from your craft. You can also leave those negative emotions on the stage and perform a song about it.

❀

Even when I was extremely open at the onset of a relationship, at the end of it the person used my drag as a weapon to hurt and attempt to shame me.

❀

Brace yourself. It is not easy being a drag impersonator and looking for a date. Dating alone is difficult enough, much less being a drag impersonator. The major issues with people dating drag impersonators and impersonators is any possible stigma they have about gender non conformity and what they may perceive it to mean for you as a person. They determine their standing within the community; through the rumor mill or what does it mean by dating an entertainer. Be clear about what they can expect. How does your drag relate to your daily life? How do you identify both in and outside of drag? How frequently do you entertain? People fear when they do not know the reality of a situation, so they fill in the blanks with outlandish ideas. Do not let them put words in your mouth or paint pictures of you with no basis. Just be very frank about who you are and what they can expect from that part of your life. Some people still will not accept it and that is fine. Dita Von Teese once said, "You can be the ripest, juiciest peach in the World, and there's still going to be somebody who hates peaches." Do not let it bother you. Thank them for not wasting your time and move on.

❀

When I first start dating a guy, I do not tell him I do drag on the first date unless somehow it is brought up in conversation. I want him to get to know me for the real me first, to show him my drag life is not what he is actually going to be dating. If we make it to more dates, then I disclose. The date is over and I am move on if they have a big issue with it. Life is too short to dwell on someone's lack of understanding, fear, or whatever hang up they have about dating a performer. There will be someone out there to support you as a performer.

❀

Not everyone is in to drag and that is okay. Negative or destructive comments have more to do with where the other person is in their own life. You are not going to change them and you should not change yourself for them.

❀

I know many impersonators that struggle finding a guy who is okay with drag and I know that can be disheartening. One thing I suggest is always be up front about it. If they do not like you for you then they are not "the one." Now for kings, I have never found a girl that was not okay with it, but I would apply the same rules.

❀

I tell possible romantic partners right away. That way, it is less likely that any negative reaction will be emotionally damaging. Other than that, my advice would be to seek romantic partners within communities of people that you know will accept your drag.

❀

BE UPFRONT. It is so important to keep the lines of communication open with whomever you date! Tell them right from the beginning and do not take it personal if they are weird about it. Too many people will love you just the way you are to keep fretting over someone who thinks they know the world. You are a beautiful, handsome, stunning brand of royalty and no mere peasant can tell you what is what.

❀

Not everyone is capable of dating a drag impersonator. It takes a strong and confident kind of man and they are hard to find. You need to improve your survival skills, as I mentioned before, and suck it up. It is not always going to be a happy ending. You are going to date a lot of different guys or girls that will react in all different ways. Prospective dates may say or do things that hurt your feelings when they learn about your Divadom. It is not a perfect world and I would not candy coat the subject of drag and dating. Just enjoy yourself and be confident in the knowledge that you deserve the best and eventually he or she will come along. I am living proof!

❀

Invite them to a show. If they cannot handle it, next! They are not for you. Plain and simple.

❀

Know that this is not everyone's cup of tea. Especially with female illusionist, even if you are perfect at keeping your drag persona separate from yourself, some cannot handle it. That is okay, because the ones who can handle it, that is someone worth their weight in gold. It is a lot to swallow; drag is so much more than an illusion in the face. It is the costumes, the traveling, dealing with two personalities, and drunk individuals at most shows (who feel like they own your attention for a period). If you are popular and well known in and out of face, sometimes it can feel like you are never "off."

❀

If you are going to date someone and you perform, you will need to be open and honest. The person should be accepting and supportive of you. If they are not or have negative feedback or not respecting you, there is an easy answer, find someone who does.

❀

Not setting yourself up is very hard to prevent, especially with dating. Emotions are rampant at this point. I would suggest honesty. Be upfront in the VERY BEGINNING. That way, you would not have to be that disappointed if things do not work out.

❀

I always let them know I am a drag impersonator up front and explain to them that they are dating me. If anyone gives you destructive comments, they are not worth your time. Nobody deserves disrespect.

❀

When you are an entertainer things are a bit different. You should always take your time before committing to a relationship. They could make or break you. You need to take your time and make sure that both sides are completely supportive.

❀

If you ever date someone that cannot accept the fact that you do drag, do not take any offense to it. Some people are so narrow-minded that they cannot see past their own image. If someone cannot accept your passion, "Be you, do you, and love who you are enough to call it quits."

❀

I have been with my partner for ten years. If they want you, they will want you in or out of drag. I think it is important not to sexualize your drag. Treat it as a career in "Theatre." Hang up your costume when you come home. When you sexualize the drag, you blur the line of sexuality for yourself and for your partner.

❀

Any potential mates should be made aware from the start. It takes a strong confident person to date a drag performer. Do not tolerate negative comments just to "get laid" or because you tired of being alone.

❀

If they will not take this part of you now, chances are they would not like something in the future. It goes back to being yourself and being happy with one's self

❀

I would rather be single than deal with someone else's issues!

❀

I have been that person; I would not ever date a drag impersonator. I thought it was nasty. I met an impersonator and my world changed. You have to see the inner side of who they are and remove those negative feelings, because at the end of the day they have the same body parts. If you are afraid to tell them, wait until feel it is right. You never know, that one person could still be your one and only.

❀

I am very upfront about my performer side right off the bat before I emotionally attached myself. It is part of who I am. I try my best to educate on what it is exactly I do. If they still do not like it, it is their loss, not mine. That is what you need to remember.

❀

If you find yourself wanting a relationship, first tell them you are an impersonator and you are not that person out of drag. Honesty is always first and for most the best way to go. You also need to let that person know that onstage it is all about acting and nothing more and that it is a job and the way you make money. Who you are offstage is the true you.

❀

Not everyone will like you and that is okay. The right person will love you for who you are.

❀

Be upfront and honest. Do not live a fantasy that everybody is going to accept you for who you are. It might bother someone that you want to date seriously. They need to know. Maybe they can accept it, maybe they cannot, but do not fall in love until you are sure it is right. I went through the same situation. Unfortunately, when they found out it became an abusive relationship, ending with me having both a broken nose and a broken heart.

❀

Be open and honest. Lay out who you are. Give them a chance to ask and be educate. If they give you a negative reaction or are not accepting maybe there not the one

❀

I would never date someone who could not accept my career. It really is such a strange thing to judge someone over a job. I am paying my bills and I am not breaking the law. If you cannot get into it, "Toodles."*

* A shortened Anglicized version of the French phrase à tout à l'heure which means goodbye.

❀

It is hard sometimes when you date someone that in the drag business. You will have to listen to the good, bad, and ugly of how they see themselves and others see them. It is always good to hear the positive things, but be strong enough to hear the negative as well.

❀

I think one of the firsts dates should be to a drag show. Then you can gage their reaction to your craft to see if they are not open minded or able to see the art in it. It is a good way to gauge if they would support you. There are people who can understand that when you are in a dress, you are a female; when you are out of drag, you are boy. I could see how people would not accept someone if they are always a drag impersonator never a boy. There are open-minded people, find someone to love all of you. Show them your heart and mind. The people worth loving will remain in your life; the rest, do not waste your time.

❀

This is something entertainers go through who has not started their career/hobby already in a relationship. Many people will be insecure about you being an entertainer; it is not worth trying to explain it to them or be patient. So many people out there will love you and accept you for you for your passion.

❀

Make sure they are familiar with female illusion. If not, make sure it is a discussion. They will either support it or not support you. The discussion should definitely be before you are emotionally attached; that way it is not much of a sting.

❀

Never let anyone snuff your passion out, if your passion is drag and entertaining. If it is a new relationship, in the early stages, invite them to a show. Let them see what you do, and maybe you can change their mind.

❀

I would only tell them about my doing drag once the dating was becoming a relationship. If I got a negative reaction or comments, I would not respond back negatively. I never tried to defend my drag. I would always leave them with a positive comment about them and wish them well.

❀

Have not yet had an "out of the business" relationship since drag, but have dated within the community (no other impersonators, but bar staff, etc.).

❀

Be honest with yourself and with the potential date.

❀

My fiancé and I have very different passions. Mine happens to be drag. At first, he wanted nothing to do with that scene, but he feels the joy it brings me, he has become more involved. Be patient.

❀

Well it is often hard. I get confused with being a real girl and dating someone. I would rather be alone and have booty calls than date someone.

❀

I think it is important to go into any romantic endeavor (whether you are a drag impersonator or not) with little to no expectations or baggage. You are meeting a new person. If you are scared and expect someone is not going to be okay with your drag, guess what, "they are probably not going to be okay with it." Go in confident. You do not need to be running your mouth endlessly about your drag, but you also should not hide it. It should really be a non-issue. If you are confident in what you do and excited to go on a date and meet a new person all will be well at the end of the day.

❀

Try not to date outside your social settings. Look for the people that are a fan of drag. Find the ones that appreciate it as an art form and know you out of drag and not trying to be a woman. Be upfront and honest from the beginning. Tell them all your tea before the first date so there are no surprises. This will eliminate heartache.

❀

Truth is #1 in starting a relationship. You must be open about your alter ego. If they cannot accept it, then they were never meant to be yours to begin with.

❀

I believe in "full disclosure." In search of possible dates, one must first "feel them out" to determine how they feel about drag. If this yields a positive response then go for it!

❀

Being upfront with anyone you are interested in is key for me. Give them the opportunity to decide if they want to move forward with you. Do not draw them in and then blindside them. If you want honesty then you bring that to the table from the start.

❀

Drag has its ups and downs, but it should not define who someone is. Everything in life has its difficulties; it does not define whom we date or how we date.

❀

Sometimes, relationships with drag entertainers can indeed work and stand the test of time. Two of my nearest and dearest have been together for twenty years today. They are still as much in love now as they were back when they first met.

❀

BE UP FRONT AND HONEST. Those are the best relationships. You are not setting yourself up for a reaction you may not like by hiding it from them.

❀

Let me say, "An entertainer should never date anyone they have met while performing." It does happen, but it usually ends badly. We should always "appear" to be available, but never actually "be available." When explaining what you do to a potential mate, you should be honest and up front from the very beginning. Tell them, "You enjoy entertaining and it is a profession; it does not define who you are." You should also make sure to ask if they are not able, and more importantly willing, to accept that part of you. If this potential mate has a jealous streak, allowing them sit in the audience to watch you perform is a bad idea. These are all things you want to find out BEFORE you get involved in a new relationship. If the reaction is not a positive one, the worst way to handle it is with anger. Not everyone will understand and you cannot expect or make them understand. You will have to accept their view even if you do not like it. You have to decide where you want to go with it.

❀

Hmm - There is no real way to prepare someone about dating an impersonator. If they do not know from the start, it will not take long for them to find out. If you think it can be something special it is good to be up front ... I have dated a couple of guys that had no clue, but though it was not something they would always go to see, they will support me.

❊

Never let someone else define you. You define the person you want to be in life. Too much energy in life is spent worrying about "what some person you are dating, will think of you." Believe me, I look at the things I changed in life for someone I do not even date anymore and wonder, "Why was I too insecure to stand up for myself?" No more, I now own my own life.

❊

When you prepare yourself for a negative response, you will probably find one. We always want to prove ourselves right. Go in with open eyes, an open mind, and allow yourself to be surprised. I always say that 99% of our relationships do not work out; but we only need the 1% that do. The rest are a learning process for both of to become the person you need to be for the correct partner.

❊❊

DRAG411's DRAG Memorial page on DRAG411.com

DRAG411

DRAG Memorial
Since 2010

For Now They Dance On A Far Grander Stage

> "Relationships require both parties to equally participate for success. Many people take far more than they give. It takes two people to create a relationship, but only one to destroy it."
>
> Todd Kachinski Kottmeier

Chapter Five

❁❁❁

Dating, The Aftermath
"How do handle a partner that decides they are struggling to accept you as an impersonator?"

Note: To maintain the integrity of this project, I did not edit most of the postings to allow the message sent in, to be in the actual words of the impersonator. I left them anonymous to allow the reader to understand them without pre-conceived bias.

❁

Before you state,

"This is what you will do for me to make me happy, ask yourself… do you spend an equal amount time and energy making them equally happy?"

Few do, because they spend so much time worrying more about their own happiness. Invest in your relationship before you ask your relationship to invest in you!

❁

Talk to them. Perhaps many of their issues have solutions. Are they insecure; do you make them insecure? Do you do it on purpose? I know I am guilty of giving my drag more quality time than I gave my partner. I told him, "Drag is my passion," forgetting "he needed to be my passion too. There is a reason the term "balancing act" extends far beyond a circus term.

❁

It is very important that they accept you as a partner, first and foremost. The struggle will usually be there, but sharing with them your adventures may trigger them to be more accepting and inviting. You do not necessarily live as the character. This "acting role" allow you the opportunity to release and vent. Just ensure you allow them to take part in your life as the impersonator, so they can experience it as well. The invitation is important. They typically have an "A-HA" moment so they can enjoy sharing the spotlight with you (and realize that you are still you).

❀

Talk it out. If your partner really loves you then he/she should want to see you happy and doing the things that make you happy.

❀

Be slow patient. Respect them for communicating their feelings and fears with you. Talk it through; ask for their problem.

❀

Lay everything out on the table for both of you. If you truly care for each other, you will find a solution, even if it means that you might take a break just to reconnect.

❀

If you love someone, you can accept anything that they do that does not involve hurting people or illegal. If you cannot then you do not love them.

❀

My partner had never ever went to a drag show, until she met me. I would never disrespect her in such a way. She now performs and partakes in choreography with me.

❀

Do not force it on them.

❀

If my drag side is a problem in a relationship, then it is not the relationship.

❀

When I started dating my boyfriend, he was unsure how he would feel about seeing me onstage as a woman. I gave him time to accept it. He came to my show and saw how happy it made me, which in turn made him happy. He also loves being a part of the community and seeing the "behind the scenes." Give them time to see how happy it makes you.

❀

Explain this is your passion and desire. Involve them as much as possible in your concepts and planning. Let them know their input is VERY important and LISTEN to hear their specific concerns.

❀

Do not budge. If being an impersonator makes you happy, they will support you. Your happiness should be more important to them then what others perceive or their own hang-ups. If you have an open conversation with them and they still cannot handle it, your happiness is not a priority. Get out of that relationship. If your happiness is their priority, they will be open to getting around it.

❀

Ask, "What are your struggles." Maybe they feel like you are spending a lot of time at the clubs and traveling instead of spending enough quality time with them. It might be something you can fix. If it is because they are uncomfortable dating a performer, it is time to cut ties and move on.

❀

Talk. Talk. Then talk some more. Let them ask questions. Give them honest feedback. Let them tell you how they feel. The root of the issue may have nothing to do with drag.

❀

If they are struggling with it either invite them to a show and let them see how happy it makes you or tell them that they do not have to come to shows if they do not want to. If drag is important to you and makes you happy then it is up to them if they want to stick around.

❀

I would weigh the costs and benefits of the relationship; is it worth giving up drag for the relationship. My mantra is, "take me for whom I am or not at all."

❀

Ask questions. Figure out what it is. Communication is SO important in any kind of relationship, and here it is even more so. Someone who cares for you will want you to do what makes you happy, no matter how they feel about it. If it is that big an issue for them, consider if you really want to stay in it. Will they change? Will they understand? Would you be willing to stop doing what you love for their convenience? Weigh your options and go from there.

❀

They will accept you for who you are.

❀

It is very difficult because you decide to become a woman for you, but you may fall in love with someone who wants you to be the person you are off the stage. Often it becomes violent; it did with me. He could not deal with his sexuality, we fought constantly, and I was a battered wife. They wired my jaw and I could no longer perform. If he could not have me, no one would. It was a very frightening time of my life. I will never we live it again; stand your ground and be your true self. Love will come to you. He broke my jaw but it did not work. I immediately went to work on a new act using two puppets, music, and myself. I called it, "Natasha Richards and the Jaw Breakers." I was a ventriloquist for six weeks while I healed. It was the most empowering thing I have ever done. People still ask me to this day, "how are the jawbreakers?" The little puppets are in my hope chest, so I will never forget.

❀

My partner has been extremely supportive. He would take my clothes to bedazzle them while I was a work. If your partner is not as supportive, you have to talk to each other about it. If they cannot accept it, maybe it is not meant to be. You should not have to choose between the two.

❊

Best thing first is to talk dealing with a partner struggling with you as an impersonator. Some people cannot set boundaries with their drag, so their partner never feel like partners. Have a life together outside of the bars if that is the case. Not every conversation has to be about the next show, contest, or pageant. I am also married to an impersonator, and even for us, sometimes we need a break from drag and anyone who knows us because of it.

❊

You have to decide what is more important to you, a relationship or significant-other? Sometimes you get both and sometimes you do not. It really depends on the person.

❊

My identity as an entertainer has become a huge facet of my life. If they cannot handle it, they are not the person for me.

❊

It is important to know if drag is a hobby or an integral part of your identity. Figuring out its significance in your life will help you to decide your boundaries and expectations for your partner. For me, drag is such an important part of my life that I cannot imagine having a partner not willing to support me. However, for others, the idea of a partner never coming to a show is no big deal. Take time to think about what you need and communicate those expectations to your partner. Ask them about their needs as well.

❊

In our careers, we sometimes come to the fork in the road that it is their career or their spouse. I have had to remind people I have dated, if they truly love me than they will not have an issue with it. If they have an issue them they do not "love all of me." It goes back to the Bernard Baruch quote, "Be who you are and say what you feel, because those who mind don't matter and those who matter don't mind."

❊

Try to be as understanding as possible. I want happiness, we all do. I would wish them the best if were unable to find middle ground. We all deserve to be happy in a relationship.

❊

Balance. Practice to juggle or be willing to drop the ball.

❊

Maybe they do not understand your position and a good discussion is always best. However, if they cannot accept you at all in what makes you happy, how can you be sure that it will be a happy relationship? Support is very important.

❊

Sometimes, you will face hardships in relationships where your partner cannot accept you do drag. It is simple. It happens. You have to realize that if someone truly cares about you, then they can accept anything that makes you more comfortable with your own life. Do not accept anything less than your soulmate in a relationship. If they cannot handle the truth, then they do not deserve it, either.

❈

Explain to them "all the stuff you do for them that is equally as important to their life, as drag is to your life." Many impersonators realize, they ask far more from their partners then they ever give back to them. Sad.

❈

Get rid of him or her.

❈

I do not want partners trying to change me so I give that same respect back. If they cannot handle it, they are free to go, no hard feelings.

❈

Communication is the key to success

❈

Separate!

❈

You simply have to ease them in to it. The struggle is "true love will look past things, control will bring you down." If they cannot understand who you are and what you do then honestly they are not for you. Do not be in a controlling relationship.

❈

Communication is the key in any relationship. Have an open candid conversation about their concerns and your feelings towards it. If they TRULY love you, they will find a way to work through their issues.

❈

If they cannot accept what you love, then they are not the one. Plain and simple. It may be tough but they learn to love what you do or they can hit the road.

❈

It is hard sometimes to watch someone you care about, get onstage looking and acting another gender. Make them part of the transformation.

❈

If they cannot like all aspects of who you are, they are not the one for you. Let them go.

❈

If they are struggling with you as an impersonator, in the first place, why should you change yourself? Move on.

❈

Sit them down and talk. Open communication is key to a healthy relationship. In order to survive with each other, find common ground help them understand find out what is bothering them and try and adjust set boundaries and ground rules to help them feel comfy always introduce them and make them feel included

❀

If they cannot accept the drag side of me, they do not accept me. I am not two different people; I am one person. Drag brings out my creativity and love for the craft. If I have to hide that for someone then I am not being real and that means they cannot handle me...

❀

Leave them. Not worth my time.

❀

I have been in this situation a few times. If that person cannot accept you for who you are and what you love to do, then maybe it is not the best fit for you. I would ask my partner if my drag was the only struggle in our relationship. Maybe you can tell why you enjoying doing drag and see if they understand.

❀

A partner is your better half ..your equal. If a person cannot be those things then there live for you was never as true as they believed. It will open your eyes to the hearts of the people in your life.

❀

No idea. I am lucky to have a wonderful man who accepts me as an entertainer.

❀

For many partners, it is not always the performing that they have a problem with, it is the drama within the community, which can taint their views of you as an entertainer. Never try to force your partner into going to shows, or being a drag wife/husband. Never do anything out of their presence that you would not want getting back to them (because it always will). If your partner is completely unsupportive, but performing is a big part of who you are, then find a mutually beneficial compromise. If they berate you for being an entertainer, re-evaluate the relationship.

❀

Keep on keeping on. They knew before we became partners. I let them struggle through it on their own.

❀

They can struggle at someone else's house.

❀

Wow. Keep the two separate, if possible. This could mean no support from the partner during the creation of the next performance. A very lonely place sometimes.

❀

I remind myself that it is their struggle, not mine. If someone I am dating has issues with what I do, I ask myself if I am willing to change a very fundamental part of who I am in order to maintain that relationship.

❀

It was not meant to be; why drag it out? It is better to let go before it gets worse. If it is meant to be, than that person will come back to you.

❀

Some folks are just not comfortable with drag and probably never will be. They do not understand it and most importantly, they do not want to understand it. Drag is merely a form of creative expression, possibly your profession, and those things really should have nothing to do with your personal relationships. Try presenting it to them in that way. It is one aspect of your life. Let your partner know that they can be as much or as little involved in it as they would like. They still need to support you and support your decision in doing what you love. Talk it out with them because the issue may not even be your drag; it may be that your spending too little time together or the way you act towards them when you are in drag. However, there are reasonable and unreasonable issues. It is up to you to set those boundaries to decide what you can tolerate and what is intolerable. It is very hard to change the mind of another. This person may not be the right person for you. Try to talk with them, but always remember that action speak louder than words.

❀

They should love you and appreciate you for what, and who you are. If they are dating you, they knew what they were getting into. If they decide it is too much for them, you need to figure if your drag or your boyfriend is the most important to you. When you decide which one is more important, drop the other one.

❀

If you feel they are worth it, try to understand their side before you lash out or bail. Find out what is truly causing the trouble. Is it friends teasing them, have you have changed, family issues, or do they truly dislike drag? You cannot help them understand or accept if you do not take the time to understand their struggle. When you hit the root cause* you can decide what is next for you.

* *A root cause is an initiating cause of either a condition or a causal chain that leads to an outcome or effect of interest. Commonly, root cause is used to describe the depth in the causal chain where an intervention could reasonably be implemented to improve performance or prevent an undesirable outcome.*

❀

Your partner should try his or her best to understand why you are doing drag. Tell them why you do it; either you do it for fun or as a job. If your partner does not like it, try slowly to include them. Explain why you do it. If they love you, they should not have a problem.

❀

Always be sensitive to their needs and realize this is their own personal issue and not yours. Try to include them and have them at performances (if they feel okay with it). That way they can see first hand how the work is done. Invite them backstage. This may help them see the transformation as it happens. Have them help with you with the removal process, so they feel you are still the same person. Some people tend to forget that the person they love is underneath all that drag.

❀

Any relationship worth having is worth fighting for, but alas, not everyone can handle the ups and downs that come with being a drag entertainer. To me, any partnership would include my other half accepting that part of me; just as they accept "I am gray as a mule and that my eyes are green."

❀

COMPROMISE. Listen to their struggles with it and try to come up with a solution. If in the end that does not work then maybe it was not meant to be. You need to do in life what makes YOU happy. Someone will accept and be able to handle that aspect of your life eventually.

❀

Once again, I have been blessed not to have to have had to deal with this, but I have seen other's struggle. How to handle the situation strongly depends on how serious you are in the relationship and the risks you are willing to take. It all comes down to a choice at that point. You can walk away from the relationship to peruse your drag career or you walk away from the career to maintain your relationship. I personally do not believe one should have to choose between the two, but I am aware of how unrealistic that is.

❀

You will have to choose between your career and your man if they are struggling with your drag. Figure out if he is worth it.

❀

Be honest and have honest discussions. I personally have problems even getting a date sometimes because they expect that as a female impersonator, I should be feminine. Now the fact that I lean towards the masculine end does not bother me, but it does ruin the compartmentalization of other people and shatter their perceptions. For someone to be right for you, they will have to accept the coin as a whole and not which side they like. Talk it out and try to work it out if you want it to work. Both people will have to try.

❀❀

The following section I shared from the book, "The Official, Original Drag Handbook," on Relationships.

Makeup has a distinct smell recognized by a man raised around many sisters or perhaps a sloppy mother. For a gay man, the smell of makeup is often like the telltale signs of a kitty litter box, of a cat owner trying to hide their feline child. This chapter has nothing to do with female impersonators. It is a tribute to the secret army of benefactors that complement performers spiritually, emotionally and often without reserve.

Creating this chapter taught me more about myself than any chapter in this book. Do not get me wrong, I am not a female impersonator. The thought of it not only scares me. "Me in a dress" would terrify my neighborhood.

Do not get me wrong, I am not one of the men that have a female impersonator on his resume of relationships (1). Not because I did not want them, but most likely most of them were smart enough to not want me. Researching this chapter consolidated many of the stereotypes I had set in my brain from a long history of working with and employing these performers.

(1). Updated: Dated Angel gLamar in 2012 for a year. We both barely survived.

In this chapter, it is not the strengthening of the stereotypes that I wish to explore with much detail. I want to spend time discussing the revelations of what makes their relationships with men far beyond expected conforms of my stereotypes and of my preset rationalization of their relationships.

Dating someone that performs as a female impersonator takes a special man. He has to be mentally alert to handle situations where many people would fail. He has to be able to explore life through his boyfriend's eyes, without reservation and judgment. He has to be willing to spare closet space, room around the sink, with his best pay off at the end of the night... is seeing the light in his boyfriend's eyes reflecting the happiness he shares in that relationship.

I lived in a home with more sisters than any man should ever have to tolerate, run by a matriarchal grandmother that created my mother, that ran our home. The smell of estrogen in the air would choke you as the smell of a cadre of females past puberty shared the same menstrual cycle. The side benefit of becoming a gay man was the knowledge I would no longer have to tolerate a cluttered sink of blow dryers, curling irons, hair spray cans, and random bottles of makeup scattered across the bathroom with jubilee.

The exciting part of becoming a gay man was no longer having to tolerate drying pantyhose dangling down from the shower, having to watch my sisters practice dance routines, and listening to the same damned songs over and over again. As a gay man, I fit the stereotype of thinking, "I would never date a female impersonator. If I wanted to date a girl, I would have remained straight."

There are two types of people, I thought, that date female impersonators. The straight man that believes that dating a female impersonator justifies him still being straight. The other is a mild, meek, and submissive gay man tagging behind the performer, carrying seven cases of changing clothes and makeup.

This is the average stereotype of the average gay man, but this is a book about exploring averages. The word average, by its true nature, determines that 99 % of the people do not agree with the conclusion. The math on that determines that 50% of each response is either for or against the conclusion, henceforth the word average.

When I was younger, thinking I was a straight man, hanging out with friends in cleverly titled gay bars like Old Plantation, Rene's, El Goya, and The Carousel I found myself fascinated by the groupies hanging around Kim Ross, Tiffani Middlesexx, Joey Brooks, and Gilda Golden. I am confident my stereotype developed during those informative years.

A male perspective forces us to believe someone surrounded by enthusiastic adoration cannot help themselves but to be sexually tempted. We watch growing up, a legion of movie stars along with rock and roll performers destroy their relationships and marriages, in search of sexual gratification of someone tossing themselves at their feet.

It would not be a far reach to believe my mind assumes this behavior repeats in the gay culture. It would not be a far reach in my mind to believe many of the people in the throng of admirers 'were guys getting sexual gratification from bedding cross-dressers and transsexuals.'

During that period of my life, the group of female impersonators around me encompassed performers that were boys offstage, some were prostitutes, and a few actually returned the adoration of the straight man with their own fetish of being excited by landing a man that claimed he was straight.

The second groups of drag boyfriends were these meek and mild mannered men scurrying through the bar behind the performers. Maybe part of my stereotype had to do with my own over the top, Infamous Todd persona. I knew that no self-respecting performer would want to date a person like me, just the thought of us rolling through the grass chasing a misplaced microphone seemed silly for both parties.

38.88% of the performers declared that their significant others did not realize they performed as an impersonator when they first met.

> "If you do not like your job,
> use all your free time to find another one.
> A job is not a career. Careers define journeys.
> Jobs only pay bills. Jobs are a walkway;
> careers are the destination."
>
> Todd Kachinski Kottmeier

Chapter Six

❀❀❀

"Not every impersonator notifies their job of their persona as an impersonator; often they just find out. For the reader struggling with negative comments flowing from their job, managers, or customers... what advice can you offer? Remember, not everyone lives in a community with tons of jobs, so just quitting each time is not an option for them. Most of America, you can still be legally fired. This is a complicated question with no easy answers. I am hoping many of you can help them."

❀

I have a normal job. I keep them separated, but eventually they find out. I never let the haters get to me. I am author too. When my boss found out, I gave her a signed copy of my book. She is proud of my book. I am proud to have her as a boss. She protects me. Find your allies at your job. They will protect you too.

❀

I do not just come right out and just share what I do in my professional environment, but I would not necessarily hide it as well. Remember, you are not that character at work and must maintain professionalism. There is a time and place for everything. Do not feel you necessarily need to hide it. It is okay to build a bit of a wall around yourself to protect your "image" as well as your employment. This can be even more difficult in a smaller community because let us face it, everyone talks. I think it is important to remember you are at your job to provide a service, and it is not necessarily your stage. Of course, you are performing to a different tune. Your efforts in the work place may be better accepted if you make that your job the main focus. Baby steps are a key factor, as well as being careful as to what information you share with those that surround you. Give it time... baby steps.

❀

Invite them to a show. Let their negativity fuel your passion.

❀

Just nonchalantly tell them it is extra income and you can have a lot of FUN with your friends experimenting with different styles and performances. Remember, THAT is a job, so remain professional. Ask THEIR advice about something every now and then, so they feel included and important (no one says you have to use it).

❀

Be self-sufficient; it trumps drag every time. With coworkers they are that coworkers, not friends. Carry yourself in a way in which you were hired. Hired as Michael then serve them him. Michelle is a part of you. She is not who you are. Safe guard that part of life.

❀

If your job finds out and people share negative comments, go to HR (Human Resources) department. Harassment is harassment no matter how you look at it

❀

Remember to keep your personal life "personal." If it seems frowned upon by co-workers or employers just make sure it does not interfere with your ability to do your job and ensure them of it. Do not call in sick to make a show. For most of us, drag is not what pays the bills.

❀

If you are a strong, hard worker that gives 110% to your job, then what you do outside of your job should not be a problem. If your performances or nightlife causes your work to suffer due to lack of energy on the job or being late or calling out, they should fire you.

❀

Know your company policies. Many companies have nondiscriminatory policies that may not protect you as a performer but can protect you from harassment. Try not to engage with those bulling you. Engaging them, from my experience, generally makes this worse.

❀

It is a tough question to answer. Just play it safe. Have two social media accounts to separate your drag life from real life. Unfortunately, bigots are everywhere and work with us as our managers and bosses. Do not make it easy for them by separating your two very different lifestyles.

❀

I am lucky; I met my employer while I was in drag. She actually hung a flyer of mine in our breakroom. Not everyone has that support. We need to adjust schedules for shows. Decide how open you can be. Maybe you can just tell them you have another part-time job or that you are an entertainer, but do not give more details.

❀

Tell your managers and even your customers, "it is something you would not like to discuss." I live in an "at will" state. I know they can fire me at any time with no further explanation. but my life outside my job is nobody's business.

Always remember, as Jynxx Monsoon said, "Water off a ducks back*." Many negative comments come from a lack of understanding. Do not be afraid to change the topic. You can also turn to that one friend who is always there for support in times like this.

* Actual cited quote,

> *"That's my gift. I let that negativity roll off me like water off a duck's back."*
>
> George Foreman

❁

It is so funny you ask this question about having a "9 to 5 job" and the employer knowing about your transition. In high school, I began teaching as a ballroom dance teacher; I had the job for seven years. I was trained to be able to teach men and women in case you got a couple. Now fast forward to me now thinking about going back to Ballroom Teaching. I would have no choice but to teach as a woman as opposed to me teaching as them a man. It is more accepting now. I hope that if I went back to Arthur Murray they would respect my decision by hiring me according to my ability to dance, teach, and sell lessons. I was ALWAYS top "Male Dance Teacher" and look forward to getting "Top Female Dance Teacher!" Should be interesting; I will keep you posted!

❁

Point out popular movies or pop culture references. While they might not all directly relate to your personal identity as an entertainer, enjoyable movies help people feel like they can relate to you, whether they can or not. Usually if you point out anything from Too Wong Foo, to Mrs. Doubtfire, to Connie and Carla, Dr.A.G. from Shakespeare, or anything campy or comedic, people will feel as though they have a better understanding and hopefully be a bit less concerned about taping your breasts or tucking your balls.

❁

HR is usually an option, though most likely the last one. Most people put down what they do not understand. Help them understand. Invite them to a show. Explain what you do and why you do it. There are still people living under rocks, help them see the light.

❁

Tell your managers and even your customers, "it is something you would not like to discuss." I live in an "at will" state. I know they can fire me at any time with no further explanation. but my life outside my job is nobody's business.

❁

I have also been quite fortunate here as well. I guess my longevity, being a good coworker, and friend has bought me much grace in this arena.

❁

Most places have an open door policy and a number you can call to anonymously to report harassment.

❁

Here is the thing about a job; they want you to let them know what is up just as much as a partner does. No one likes being blindsided, so let your job know immediately. Keep in mind also that managers, customers, other associates, discussing your private life is not okay. If it is an issue, tell someone above your boss. If that person does not like it, go higher. At some point, it does become discrimination and someone is going to catch on to that.

❀

I do not mix my drag life with my profession. It is very important to keep them both professional and separated.

❀

Keep your personal life personal. Do not discuss what you do afterhours with coworkers. If they approach you about it, just let them know you do not discuss your personal life.

❀

I think we should all keep our personal lives separate from our professional lives. It is not very hard to do. I have done it on many occasions. If they find out and feel like you are being singled out, I suggest keeping your chin up and reminding yourself that are at work to pay for a life you love (hopefully).

❀

I try to keep my lives separate when I work away from performing. I keep separate social network accounts for my drag persona and my real self. When they discovered me, I did not receive negative feedback. I would advise others to be professional and do their best to keep things professional and separate.

❀

I have avoided this by just telling my job, "I am a dancer."

❀

I generally do not bring my drag life to work. Some jobs love it. However, with the need to be professional at work I do not tell customers that I am a drag impersonator. I get to know the managers and staff before I let them in my life like that.

❀

I would record everything that happens and consult with a lawyer. Discrimination or harassment is a lawsuit. If you cannot do this, I would suggest finding another path to follow. It is a changing world; we must stand up for who we are and ourselves. If we do not, our kids will not.

❀

The year is 2016, and we still see harmful discrimination. The world is a sinful place and it still causes this community to falter. However, jobs and careers are cutthroat for everyday people. If you ever face discrimination in the job force, know it is going to get better. Work each day with a smile on your face and realize you are the only one paying your bills; the haters are not. Keep your head held high, and love yourself. I love you, so you should love you. Do not ever let anyone cause you to quit a job that you have worked hard for, just because the person does not accept minorities.

✿

I live in Canada, so the employer would be responsible for shutting this down at a workplace level. You should not face any discrimination. If you are in another country, I would try approaching it the same as you would any other extracurricular activity. Explain to them, it is no different from community theatre or other hobby. Again taking the sex out of drag will help the fearful.

✿

My advice is to perform at as many charity events as possible. I love telling people how much money I have helped raise for various community non-profits. It shuts them up real fast. You have to educate people as to what good you do in the community. A lot of the public still see drag performers as drunken hookers trying to fool straight men, which is far from the truth

✿

I try to keep work and personal life separated. If they are not willing to let you work because of something that you do in the free time, than you have you look inside of you.

✿

What you do on your own time should not reflect on your job, it is 2016. Times are changing!

✿

If you are being bullied or bashed because you told them or they found it then it's not right. Contact Proper Authority figures in the company and have the matter fixed. No place should bully anyone for who and what they do or are.

✿

There needs to be a distinction between your professional and personal life. Drag, in most cases, is personal. Not everyone needs to know about it, nor are they interested in it. I think there is a time and a place for "outing yourself." Your boss will not accept you calling in sick not every Monday because you had "a show" the previous night.

✿

Work can be hard. I have the fortune of working for one of the top companies when it comes to equality. However, you need to have some key support person that you can go to when harassed, whether it is a manager, colleague, or your HR representative.

✿

Always remember this is just a job and that you go home at the end of the show. It is best if you say nothing sometimes. Do not go into your job in drag. No matter what job you have, do it to the best of your ability. I worked outside of being a drag impersonator. Now I am a Trans*FTM. I worked through it all. I was lucky to have no major problems and if I did, they address it to me. I was honest with them so we went on about our way and did our jobs.

❀

Sadly, in some states or in the job industry you have to hide your true self to be able to keep a job and not be constantly harassed for not being you. Drag is acting, so, act. Act as straight as you can. Keep your drag life at home. Sometimes you have to live two separate lives to be able to make it in this unfair world.

❀

It is a very fine line to cross. Luckily, I am in a position where my clients and superiors accept me for who I am. If you think it is going to hurt your career, you may want to wait to divulge this to your employers. Be very careful, not everybody is open-minded. You have to be prepared to take a chance. Get involved with some organizations and help get the laws changed so we are not fired for being who we are.

❀

Be who you are and try to help them understand. Do not let them knock you down or shake you in life. You will find people who do not accept you or like you, but stay true to yourself and your beliefs. Try to educate them. If they do not want to learn, it is their loss. Remember to be always you

❀

You would hope everyone has an open mind, but we do not live in a fairy tale. If your job does not accept your after-work activities and they say hurtful stuff, ignore; it would be your best defense. I honestly do not feel like a place of work has a say in what someone does out of work. ESPECIALLY if what you do is legal. They dictate your job, not your life. Honestly, depending on what they say, I would contact the Better Business Bureau and an LGBT rights group to understand your options. Bullying is harassment... sometimes you need to take the step to show it is not okay.

❀

A retail store manager once called me a "tranny.'" I reported the incident to corporate and she got a promotion. I was lucky enough to find a job the next week, but even if I would not have found that job, no amount of money is worth my integrity. Always weigh the costs and benefits of every situation, and know your worth.

❀

I would continue working the job and if became a legal battle then I would do it. It is not fair for your extracurricular activities outside of work should not determine your work abilities.

❀

Everyone can and should be cautious of their environment and surroundings. If you work for a place known for their conservative beliefs, keep your personal life personal. Not everyone has to know everything about you. If you work for a place open to diversity, then chances they will accept you for being gay and a performer.

❀

I hope that by the time this book is published it will be illegal for you to be fired. At the end of the day, I think it is worse to hide yourself than to be harassed for being yourself. I think open dialogue and patience is key, especially if there are many work opportunities in your area! I would challenge the person reading this book, "Why do you stay in a place where you fear doing what you love?" Sometimes leaving means being far away from those you love. The wonderful thing about this world is that there are open communities who will embrace and love you. There is a bus, train, or an airplane to get you home to visit. Make "you" first always.

❀

A job is your job. Female illusion is your personal life and if it has nothing to do with your occupation, they should have nothing to say. If they bring it up, politely say it is not work related; it does not have to be discussed.

❀

Many companies have a zero tolerance policy for harassment in the workplace. Rather than trying to deal with a situation yourself, I would always recommend taking it to your HR or ethics department. Trying to handle a bullying situation on your own can often cause it to escalate, which could result in you losing your job. Taking it through the proper channels is the best way to ensure it is taken care of properly.

❀

If someone "outs" you, "Bitch, you better embrace it!" If you remain proud of what you do, it is difficult for the people you work with to taunt you about it. *"Yes, yes I am. Why you mad, boo? Is it because I am a better man than you will ever be and a better woman than you will ever get."*
*Actual Quote, "I'm more of a man then you'll ever be, I'm more of a woman then you'll ever get." By Jonathan Larson, Rent

❀

Keep it separate as long as possible If they do find out, they must have been at a show. Most of us look very different in our alter egos.

❀

I try to leave all non-work aspects of my life at home.

❀

Wow, this is not easy to answer. When they hire you at a job, it is better to let them now. Ask, "Hey, I do drag on the side. Is that a problem?" Some places will fire you. You cannot make a living from drag. It is better to keep it as a hobby and when the time is right, let your coworkers what you do. You may be surprised; there may be a huge support there

❀

They should not have to notify their job unless it violates a contract with the employer. Always try to keep your professional and personal life separated as much as possible. Educate and guide someone to understand, if they find out (and bring it up).

❈

Keep one job separated from another. If your job is so conservative and someone says they saw you or was at the bar where you were performing just say, "If I made enough money at my day job I would not have to take a second job."

❈

Your job has no jurisdiction in your private time. I have not once had a job "just find out." Unless you are in a gay friendly environment, saying nothing.

❈

If they know and have questions, it is your decision whether or not to answer. Always remember that ignorance can be dangerous. Choose your battles especially in the work place. Being defensive can be a bad thing but allowing ignorance to run you down can be too. The best choice would be to limit those discussions without being defensive or holier than thou. It is hard for some of us not to go into "Diva Defense Mode" but sometimes it is best to be honest and be ever so understanding of their ignorance.

❈

I for one do not tell my job that I do certain things like that. I keep my job away from my personal life. It is hard enough because they do know that I am gay and I did not mean for that to come up. I would just be careful when it comes to jobs.

❈

I have been fortunate (all right, even blessed) enough to have always worked with people who are *EXTREMELY* open-minded and understanding. Not everyone is as fortunate, however. To them, I offer the following advice: do not be a pushover, but take no shit either.

❈

I was fired for doing drag. Now I have my profile set to where anyone I work with is restricted from viewing my profile, I keep drag life and boy life separate, I do not discuss it, nor invite them to the shows. I keep both boy and drag profiles set to private and must approve any content someone tags me.

❈

Ouch! I am going to have to ponder this one and come back to it... Okay, if explaining to your boss that your night job does not define you or effect your day job in any way does not work, if your job is threatened by your past-time, the reality is you have to earn a living and take care of you. Therefore, you may have to decide what is more important to you, your lively-hood, or your drag.

❈

Well honey - read that company manual! Most companies are nowadays accepting of the gay community but keep in mind some jobs may find that doing Drag is a conflict of interest or as moonlighting. In which case you really learn how to hide that if you wish to continue. You make sure it does not make a bad influence on your job.

❃

Coming out as transgender or a cross-gender performer is like coming out a second time: all the fear, reservations, and consequences are there, but this time more defined. I know that some of us simply want to blend in and go about our work, but that may not be our lot in life. You may have to endure criticism, probing questions, and cold shoulders. You may have to help the company set standards regarding harassment, discrimination, and defamation. It will only help the company move forward for its own benefit. In no way did I say it was an easy road.

❃❃

> "Every family has a secret. Every person in your life has a secret. At least your secret involves glitter and cheering crowds. I bet their secret is not as fun as your secret."
> Todd Kachinski Kottmeier

Chapter Seven

Not every impersonator notifies their family of their persona as an impersonator; often they just find out. For the reader struggling with negative comments flowing from their family, what advice can you offer?

Note: To maintain the integrity of this project, I did not edit most of the postings to allow the message sent in, to be in the actual words of the impersonator. I left them anonymous to allow the reader to understand them without pre-conceived bias.

❀

I was always very careful as to what was said around me when family was around as well as making sure that all of my "impersonator" items were always packed away and out of view. With the changing of times, I realized that it was silly to hide it. As far as experiencing negative comments from family members, always approach this with a soft disposition. Not everyone will accept it, but it is important for them to understand your intentions and what it means to you. Before a judgment is passed, allow them to be involved and take part in it. Perhaps if they see how others feel about what you do and provide in a positive way, they will also see the light and respond positively.

❀

Nonchalantly tell them it is extra income and you can have a lot of FUN with your friends experimenting with different styles and performances. Ask for their ADVICE on how to improve and let the NON-constructive comments roll off your back.

❀

Open and honest from jump. I say this because at 14 I told my mother I was different and wanted to be a woman. I was put out, disowned, and put in terrible situations to take care of myself. Five years later, I went home to say hello and allow her to meet Mya, we bonded and I never looked back. People have to deal with their emotions and adjusting. You deserve your own happiness without regret.

❀

I am a performer whose family has no idea I do drag. I hide it. It takes a lot of effort, work, and is stressful. I am a performer at heart and enjoy it. I know how my family will react and that is my choice not to tell them.

❁

This one I would consider the hardest to cope with. Friends come and go but family is forever. If someone is receiving negative comments from family members, try to have a civilized conversation (as difficult as it may be). If that does not work then it IS okay to step back and let your family process what is going on

❁

My mom found out through my snooping aunt. Honestly, the best thing you can do is remind them that you love them, but their opinions are unwarranted and irrelevant. Family may be blood, but you are not required to conform to their beliefs.

❁

When you make your decision to come out as gay, you take a chance to have people not except your lifestyle. When you choose to become a performer, it is the same issue. You may have people not understand. So you have make a solid decision on what you want and everything else will fall in line as life will have it.

❁

As much as it hurts, try not to let it bring you down. As someone whose family stopped talking to them for a period of time after finding out, look to your fellow performers and friends. Sometimes your non-blood family is the ones that really have your back. If drag is a sore spot with your family try not to bring it up every day.

❁

I am always about keeping the peace. You may not want to tell your 80-year-old grandma that you duct your junk or you stuff it with a sock. If this is the case, you may not want to drop your big announcement at the family reunion. If they find out somehow, mine walked into one of my shows because someone told my mom I was performing. That went over about as well as her finding out I was gay. Did she freak out? Um, yea! I told her what I told you, I simply love to dance and express myself through music. Honestly, we have not had that conversation since. Does she know that I perform? Yes, but I choose not to wear anything that is "showy" in front of her, just to prove a point that I am grown and I do what I want! :)

❁

It is about how you explain yourself.

❁

I really do not share it with my family because I do not expect a favorable reaction. I have shared it with my sister, but given zero response from her, I guess she is uncomfortable. Only you will know when to come out.

❁

The beautiful thing about being gay and a performer is we get to choose our family. That does not mean that you have to cut ties with your biological family, but you can lean on them for the family love and support you need. Since your biological family does love you, they may in time, come around after seeing how happy it makes you.

❦

This question was asked of me many times over the years. I was fortunate enough to have a very entertaining, performing, stage loving family. My grandmother was an original rocket from Radio City Music Hall and my mother a model for Gimbel's and Macy's in New York City... my Uncle also an actor and model. He had a small part in the black and white television series "Danger Will Robinson!" I forget the name of the character, but have the footage somewhere on reel to reel. I came out when I was 16 years old after my mother took me to my first gay bar, and yes, my mother was a lesbian with three children. I guess she was on a mission, always wanted children, and then ditch the guys. It happens all the time. The other way around she saw the drag show, looked at me and said, "I bet you could do that." Sure enough, the next two weeks I got prepared and did my first talent show at 16 and a half going on 17 years old. I won and became the youngest show director I think, in the history of mankind. The owner of the bar was so proud of me and was good friends with my mother. My sister is also a lesbian with children, must have been something in the water I suppose. They are always accepting of me. I was always the consummate performer making them laugh (really making them cry) until recently. Just because mom and grandma are gone, we have kind of got our own families and caught up in our own lives. Sometimes it's not them that does not want to be around us, it's us that does not want to be around them, because we're not the person we used to be when we were just little boys or little girls. I believe that now, and I am trying harder. I want to see my nieces and nephews grow up to be strong, independent women and men... Always protecting and defending the LGBT community because that is what their family core was practically made of! I think, "Always be honest." Life is too short to be untrue to them or oneself!

❦

The family thing is never easy and out of emotion or fear, family tends to say many unfortunate things. Try to understand that it is out of fear, and that fear is because they do actually care even if it is coming out twisted and gross. A lot of times your parents, or whomever, are grappling with their own understanding of the world. Be glad you do not have that struggle, even if it hurts to be on the receiving end of theirs. Try to understand that most people are doing their best with what they think is "right." but know that you do not have to stick around and take it. Even if it is from some twisted well-meaning place, let them know that you do not need that, and you will not hang around to continue to take it. They can work out their issues on their own time. It is not for you to tolerate. Stick to your guns and they will eventually come around.

❦

One brother just wants to ignore it and not hear about it; the other prays for my salvation, and to see the light, to move away from this behavior. Both still love unconditionally and I love unconditionally in return. It works for me. I do not need to force them to acceptance. I am pleased they were not aggressively intolerant.

❀

Family is supposed to show unconditional love, remind them of this. Explain that if they love you they have to love all of you, not just the parts they like or accept.

❀

This is a tough one. I was a little nervous when my parents found out but now my dad helps me pick my music. My brother and sister-in-law are not as accepting. I tell them it is not any different from being in a play or a musical or a movie. At the end of the night, the makeup comes off and I live as a girl. I have never been interested in being a boy and never will. Stage is just a place to work through issues or to have some fun.

❀

Family is important. However, I believe that when you are being disrespected, and the support and understanding is not there, you might be able to find it among friends.

❀

Not every family will be accepting of their children doing drag, including my own. My advice would be to let them believe what they want and create your own family among your community. Anyone who cannot support you for who you are should hardly be considered family, and the definition of that word is rapidly changing.

❀

You can try, and try, and try some more, but to be very honest, sometimes family is not going to get it. That is going to hurt a lot, but I have got a secret for you: you do not have to like your family. You do not have any obligation, outside of a social norm, to please them. When you think about it, as a performer, you are not exactly a person for social norms anyway. You do not have to have toxic people in your life. Remember that.

❀

You must be willing to come out to family or else the struggle will be real.

❀

Understand that not everyone can accept this lifestyle but try to surround yourself with like-minded individuals who will support you no matter what.

❀

I have personally not gotten any negative comments from my family. I know that some have their opinion on it. You just have to stop caring about what others think. It's harder when you are young, but the older you get, the easier it becomes. You get to choose your family. I do not want to be around mean or hateful people.

The people I keep in my life are the supportive ones. The ones that are not, they see a lot less of me. I do not have time for it.

❁

My family has always been accepting of my alter ego. A lot of them have come to shows. They like to give pointers and ideas. When they say negative things, I like to remind them that it is an art form. It is self-expression. It is a way for me to be someone who I cannot always be. It is helped to get me over my shyness, bring me out of my box. It has gotten me thru a bad case of depression. I have made many new friends and a lot that I consider to be more family to me than actual blood family.

❁

My parents found out and told me it was disgusting and that I should quit. They did not ever have supportive things to say to me so I ignored them. What good would it do me to focus on someone who does not understand or care? If you love what you do, you do not need to listen to those who do not support you.

❁

Most of my family was okay with it except my mom. She never liked that I did drag and would not support any of it. Until one day, she showed up to a mother's day show surprising the hell out of me. Once she saw me, she instantly thought I was amazing. It took her 8 years to finally see me and what I love, and she did a complete 180 and is now my biggest supporter and fan. For the negativity from family, I would challenge them to come a see what I do and most of the time seeing what I do changes their mind. Family is supposed to support each other and sometimes it just takes them time to come around.

❁

It is just like coming out a second time. Give it time and they will come around. Do not let them treat you poorly or different because of it!

❁

My family did not immediately accept my choice of careers; I was kicked out as a teenager. I will not go into much detail. I will say that whatever words they used, they are just words; the words eventually fell by the wayside. What really matters in the end, are your actions. Despite their words, make sure you are always in control of your own actions.

❁

Your family may not understand your choice in performance persona, and it may be they do not know how to ask the right questions. My best advice would be reach out to those family members via an email, letter, or instant messenger. I have found that has worked best with me. Allow them the chance to ask those tough questions. If they continue to make negative comments to you, you have every right to inform them that you will not allow or listen to their inappropriate statements. They may be family, but you do not have to take their negative words or behavior.

❁

I have personally had some past difficulties with my own family. Yet in time, they learned to accept it. They finally saw how much it made me happy and how well I do, they are proud. Some are not lucky as I am, to those: hang in there, its ok. They just do not understand and these things take time. Be patient.

❀

I understand what it is like to feel afraid of your family finding out about your drag career. However, my fears died when I realized it is what I am going to do no matter what. When I told my mother for the first time, I was scared to see a reaction. However, I knew that no matter what her response was, it was not going to cause me to stop. Surprised as I was, she totally accepted it. She even went as far as to help me get ready before a show, and she even helped me get into my hip pads. What I am saying is that, sometimes we are so scared to admit what makes us happy. Our family should be accepting. If not, then we have to be strong and independent and fight for what we love. Educate people. Teach them why it is what makes us happy. You have to be an educator for those who need learning of this side of life.

❀

You cannot choose your family. You do not have to love them. Non-sexualize it for them and explain the entertainment aspect of drag. If they still cannot wrap their heads around it, do not bring it up with them or avoid them. If it is a parental situation, and you live at home, just hang in there. Soon you will go where you need to be yourself. Chances are if you are coming out as an impersonator, you are already out as a Queer person. This will not be as hard.

❀

Tell them first before they find out, it is not an easy conversation, but telling them first prevents their imagination from running wild. Many people have no experience with drag so they automatically jump to the worst stereotypes imaginable. Tell them, or even better, take them to a show and let them experience it first-hand.

❀

Every family is different. My family is split, some know and some do not. I hate to say it, but I just kind of keep quiet around the ones who do not.

❀

It is very sad that some family members cannot accept others thoughts, beliefs, or actions, but it is the way of the world. Again, you have to do what makes you happy! Live for yourself not your family! The ones who love and accept you will embrace all you do. The ones who do not accept you should not matter! It is just like politics or religion, we all have a right to our beliefs as well as others have the same right to disagree or disapprove!

❀

Personally, mine hates it when I do it, the short period of time I do it. They feel that is disgusting because I have my penis tucked in my ass. So if that is all they hate, then so be it. As for some advice, just do not talk about it around them, and eventually it gets easier, and they again will either understand and accept, or it will be something you just do not talk about.

❃

I told my family that I was gay and an impersonator at the same time. They did not care about the gay thing, the impersonator thing was much harder to handle. Again, do they need to know everything? I guess it all depends on how open people want to be with their family about all aspects of their life.

❃

You make your own family. Sometimes we lose our biological family but we gain our performer family and it can be the best gift in disguise. Family is someone that loves you unconditionally. If being a performer changes that love towards you, they are not TRUE family.

❃

I was one of the ones I did not tell my parents and I had to live two different lives. It was hard, but I did it. I was getting ready one night at home, and not knowing my mother was home, she saw me and she about died. I told her, "you ask me no questions and I will tell you no lies." My parents were the in the bible belt and our family was very well known, so my parents did not want me to get ready at their home, or let anyone they knew see me in drag. It took a while before my parents came around about everything, but they did, and it was not easy. I do not know how to tell someone about how to handle their family when it comes to this. I did tell them it was just a job even though it was more than that for me.

❃

Do not worry about it too much. If they find out, that is one less stress off you trying to hide it. It is like theatre. Tell them that you are basically an actress/actor and you are performing on a stage.

❃

Many people struggle with family members because they blame themselves. You have to make them understand it was nothing they did. A little easier now, then it was in the seventies and sixties. With the advent of different programs on television and more education, families understand. The first part of the family to start with is your immediate family; they possibly can help you get through it as long as they are educated by you.

❃

Personally, it was not always easy. Nothing you truly want in life is. With that being said, everyone comes from different walks of life. Sometimes people fear what they do not understand and hate what they do not want to learn. Try to help them learn; invite them out. If they refuse, then lift your head up and smile. One day they will come around. If not, a million people will have your back, trust me.

❃

My family honestly does not support what I do. They are Middle Eastern and my parents are rather old. They do not quite understand it. They sometimes ask why, and although they do not like it when I explain how much I love it, or show them videos of me doing it, they tend to leave me be for a few months. I suggest you explain how it makes you feel. Not everyone will support it but your family loves you. You may even want to bring them out to a show and let them see you, and see how the "fans" react to you.

❀

I have no relationship with my blood family, partly having to do with my job as a female impersonator. Living my life as a happy individual is worth far more than dealing with a toxic influence in my life because she is my "mom."

❀

Your family may not understand at first, but give them time. They might not like it, but they love you at the end of the day.

❀

Ever since I came out if the closet, I made it my mission to educate my family about all members of our community. I chose to do drag and my family showed up to my shows. You understand your family best. If they struggle with you being gay, they will not understand you personifying a female.

❀

The wonderful thing about Drag is we create our own families. Just as if you would cut a friend out of your life for being negative, sometimes you have to cut out biological family members. It is not necessarily forever, but it is your life and you would not please everyone and you do not have to. You only have to please yourself.

❀

Involve them in what you do. Send pictures, invite them to venues, and show them videos. They may not understand what it is you do, or why you do it, so make them a part of it. They still might not fully "get it," but at least they will see that you are not trying to hide it, that it is nothing to be ashamed of.

❀

I was always open with my family from the start because I am not ashamed of myself or of my doing Drag. I did get negative comments behind my back from my eldest brother and I ignored it.

❀

Invite them to see you perform. If they show up, bitch, you had better bring the most epic of fucking numbers. Make them eat everything you are serving, but do not focus on them - focus on you and your performance. If they do not want to come, it is their loss - not yours.

❀

Expressing oneself is the most relaxing medicine in this world filled with so much hatred and masking. Be free.

❀

Family is tricky, I personally moved hundreds of miles away from my family, and it's been the most amazing thing that I have ever done for myself.

❀

Mom will always love us no matter what... Dads are the hard ones to get through to. I'm sure if you sit them down and speak to them, they will be okay, and if they are not, well then, if you don't live under their roof, then **** them ... This is what is paying for your bills and rent and even their lunch or dinner whenever you take them out.

❀

Family is a hard one and I think is very similar to dealing with romantic relationships. How you express yourself creatively and professionally should really have nothing to do with your family relationships. You have to treat it as separate from your family life, no matter how much those busybody relatives try to make it a part of your relationship. Try to have an honest conversation about their concerns, but just remember that changing someone's mind is very difficult if not impossible, and is also not your responsibility. Just like with romantic relationships, it is important to set boundaries; if you need to, make a rule that there will be no talk of your drag. If they have questions, that is fine, but their opinions about your drag are irrelevant and unwelcome.

❀

I have never experienced this, but if they have a problem with you doing drag, then chances are they are not comfortable with you being homosexual. All you can do is ask them to come to a show to see you in action and get feedback from them.

❀

Either they will accept you for your job as an entertainer or they will not. Help them understand that you are not the stereotype that the news shoves in their face. Show them pictures or a video performance or invite them to a show. If they really love you, they will just let it go, and if they cannot accept you for you, then they are baggage, and you must let them live with their ignorance and live your own life.

❀

My family found out because my father followed me one night when I was supposed to be attending an extra-curricular after school activity. I was working on a "Haunted House" for the Jaycees, and one night I got ready at a friend's home to perform at a club at the age of seventeen. Once the show started, the bar was raided and closed down by my father, because I was underage. After that was the eternal fight of me saying, "Well, I am gay," and them saying, "You do not know what you are talking about." I was president of my High School class of Thespians (a drama organization in most schools). Well, it ended up with them asking me if I would see a Psychiatrist. I said "sure." Much to their chagrin, the Dr. came out of our interview and told them "I am here to help people who are unhappy to change, I can do nothing for your son for he is not unhappy, you will have to accept him the way he is. After that, all my Dad said was, "Whatever you choose to be, be the very best." The rest is history!

❀

That is not always easy, I get that. Self-acceptance is really all I can offer here. For me, my family did not take it too well. Questions like, "do you want to be a boy?", "are you transgender now?", "do you not know that will send you to hell?" Really harsh questions, but it is okay to answer them. Do not get angry and defensive. You do not have to explain every little thing, but remember where they are coming from. They do not know this side of you, and just like you, they have to learn. Be proud of you and your craft, but take the time to help your family understand. They may just come to a show. If not, you will survive.

❀

It was hard to tell my mother and father about it, but after a while, they became okay with it, and throw jokes here and there. It is all what you can handle as a person. If you cannot come out and tell your parents, then do not, or tell them when the time is right for you.

❀

I come from a Christian background, Pentecostal to be exact. The very first time I told my family that I did drag, a lot of them did not even know what it was. So after explaining it to them, they said, "if it makes you happy and pays your bills, then by all means do what you want to do. We cannot tell you what to do in life, all we can give you is advice, and it's up to you to do what you want with it." Some of my family members still to this day do not like my lifestyle, but it is simply that, MY LIFESTYLE. Not everyone in life is going to like or agree with what you do. You have to be okay with that.

❀

If they find out, the most important thing is to educate them concerning drag. Explain the art behind it. Explain the process and how it works. Removing all the stereotypes that usually come with it. Educating people is key.

❀

Most of my family knows I am an entertainer, just as they know I am trans. Has it been easy? No, but I have a better relationship with my sisters and stepmother because of it. Hang in there, it really *does* get better.

❀

It is like coming out all over again... if your family accepts you as being gay, they will come around eventually to drag. Explain to them it is an art form, not a lifestyle. For me, drag is a character I created, once offstage, I am male again. I do not let them think I want to be a female, because I do not. I am happy as a boy and want to remain one.

❀

I simply came clean about it to my siblings and they just thought I was weird but wished me well. It was my mother that I had a problem with it. When I won my first National Title, I wrote her a letter and sent an 8 x 10 of me in face, crown, and sash, but I did not tell her who it was. When she called me, she said, "I got your letter, it was very nice thank you. Why are you sending me pictures of strange men?" When I told her it was "me," she balled in hysterics. She thought I had a sex change.

Therefore, I do not suggest that method. Once again, I suggest that you be up front and honest. Explain, "It is an art form that you enjoy." Show them pictures of you in drag and explain that it is nothing more than a persona onstage and that you are still the same person you have always been. You can also show them a video if you like. Again, try not to go into this with any expectations. Prepare yourself for the worst and hope for the best.

❦

You cannot choose your family but they will always have their input. It is all in what part of the family that has an opinion. All opinions honey, are like asses; they all stink. You know whom you need to back you in your life. Sometimes this makes us grow up faster and on our own. You merely have to do the best that YOU can do for yourself.

❦

I invite my family to watch me in my performances, so they can see for themselves how much effort it takes to be convincing, and how much I enjoy doing it.

❦

Do not allow them to over sensationalize what you do. Many times, it is really not as crazy as they think or see on TV. They care and want what is the best for you, but they would not really be able to be any help to you in that regard until they actually understand what you are doing. The biggest piece of advice I can give here is to figure out what you are doing first, so that you can get to the point where your loved ones can jump on the wagon. Do not avoid it altogether, because you will end up with a wall between you and miss having the blessing of having them completely in your life.

❦❦

> "I don't have to always beat you up.
> Sometimes my friends will do it for me.
> Boo me onstage and I will have the entire audience tearing you apart. I call it audience participation."
> Todd Kachinski Kottmeier

Chapter Eight

❈❈❈

You and I know that not every single person entering a bar is "drag friendly." Every audience will have someone not into drag... having them drunk adds complications. This question is twofold. One is about the heckler harassing the reader, but more importantly, it is about the aggressive customer approaching them offstage.

Note: To maintain the integrity of this project, I did not edit most of the postings to allow the message sent in, to be in the actual words of the impersonator. I left them anonymous to allow the reader to understand them without pre-conceived bias.

❈

There will always be those hecklers. To that I say, keep talking about me... it keeps me out there. Again, not everyone is going to accept it and that is okay. Just do you. It is very important to surround yourself with those that care for you and that you care about. You do not need to lash out, and let us face it, you can always use the support. Be careful about a negative response back that would only add fuel to the fire. Allow them to their own opinions and feel free to report any harassment to those that can defuse or handle the situation on your behalf in a proper manner. Remember, you cannot be bothered by issues such as this.

❈

If drag is not what they like enough to heckle you, they should find a different bar and there is so many that are there just to see you. Focus on the positive people that are enjoying you as much as you enjoy them having fun because of you. If the heckler gets aggressive, have the person escorted out and remember it is a flaw in their character, not yours.

❈

Smile and respect everyone's opinions. Be confident in YOU. Words are words. Do not give the power over who you are and what you do. Not everyone is going to like you or your talent. So when I've listened to people say you should have done this or that, or you're as good as so-and-so, I simply smile and ask nicely,

"When are you performing next so I can come get some pointers?" Answer: "oh, I don't perform." Exactly, and smile as I walk away.

❀

In any bar that has performers, there are more times than not that the heckler will be surrounded by drag supporting crowds. They would most likely get shut down before you know what is going on. Just perform as you always do. The person would most likely be shut down before you even get offstage. If it happens, just tell the person to stop politely. If they do not, security is your next step.

❀

Most of the places I have performed in have Security, and they know their job! If a heckler is disrupting the performance, Security, with just a nod, will escort them out. If they follow you outside, DO NOT CONFRONT THEM! Go back in and talk to Security or call the police.

❀

You have to stand strong in what you do as an entertainer. What a negative Nancy has to say is just words. Remember, these people are most likely under the influence of something. So ask yourself, is responding really a good idea?

❀

Okay, my question is, if they are not into drag shows, why the hell are they there? In this case, just simply say, thank you for coming and giving your money at the door and supporting us. Enjoy the show, and I hope it is good enough that you would return.

❀

We are paid to make an ass out of ourselves.

❀

Oh, I see so many opportunities here! Impersonators with microphones can read these folks and throw some shade. I like to dance up on drag show virgins or girls not paying attention to me. I have even taken a girl's phone and dropped it in her cleavage because she was texting. I hate being ignored when I perform. I will do anything to get that attention back! If you cross the dance floor and I am on it, you are fair game to become part of my act!

❀

The first concern of the bar or club you are performing at is to keep their employees safe. Do not be afraid to tell security or the bartender about a patron that is harassing you. Nine times out of ten, they will be removed from the bar. Do not be afraid to have someone walk you to your car or wait with you for your ride. If that is not an option, talk to someone on the phone while you walk or wait, you can even put them on speakerphone. This will make someone think twice about starting something.

❀

Do not be afraid to stand up for yourself. Getting up onstage, you can expect people will be judging and deciding what they think, and if they want to tip.

That does not mean anyone has any right to harass or demean you. You are a person who deserves respect. Do not be afraid to point someone out to security or if in an unsafe or uncomfortable situation draw attention. Whether it is being louder or walking to a more central part of the bar where everyone can see what is happening, in case that person is getting too aggressive. Ask for help. Most other bar goers will not hesitate to assist if you speak up for yourself and ask for it. Bartenders and staff will throw an aggressive jackass out on their head in a heartbeat, be vocal, and stand your ground. What is to prevent them from doing it to you again, or to someone else throughout the night if you don't?

❀

SECURITY! Any bar hosting a drag show needs to have security on hand that is willing to step in, take care of the situation, and protect the performer from any harm, verbal or physical. If this is not happening, then a conversation needs to be had with management.

❀

Do not back down. There are other bars and they can leave just as they came in. Do not egg them on, but do not let them belittle you. You are a person deserving of respect, as you give, so should you get.

❀

Never find yourself alone. Surround yourself with friends and make sure you become friends with the management and security staff of the bar or venue that you are working at. If someone tries to become aggressive with you, make sure security knows about it.

❀

Most bars with entertainment or events usually have bouncers. If you are feeling harassed, on or offstage, you should report it to bar staff and have the heckler removed from the establishment. If you are afraid of harassment outside the establishment, do not travel alone. Travel with friends or ask for an escort to your destination from others.

❀

Know who has your back. If someone is making you uncomfortable, get your support system ready. Let people know what has happened, what is happening. The more people who know, the more eyes are watching, and when someone is causing trouble, that is the route you want to take.

❀

I have never had this problem, but I would not take it from them. That is the reason for security.

❀

Hecklers are attention seekers and I find that acknowledging them feeds their need. I suggest ignoring them. If you are a witty and clever person with a sharp tongue, I love seeing an entertainer bring the heckler into the show without the heckler knowing they just took part in something they despise. As for aggressive patrons, I do not know. I do not know because I am not afraid to be aggressive back. So I wouldn't have a safe answer on this part.

❀

Make friends with the security, the bartenders, bar backs, management, and go-go dancers. They will be there for you if needed. Onstage, a smile and a middle finger is always good in my book, even if it is an internal one. If you are hosting, you have a microphone. You can talk over them. If it is offstage, remember your new friends at the bar. Remember that you are wearing heels. They can inflict pain if things get out of hand.

❀

I would say keep shining. Push on and do not give hecklers a reaction. That is what they want. Show them you came to put on a show whether they like it or not. If someone harassed you offstage, I would say inform the staff or security to have them removed.

❀

I ignore people's negative comments and move quickly to a safe location.

❀

Being a straight drag ally, I have found that, for some wonderful reason, many are quite protective of me and intervene before I even realize there may be an issue. I might be a bit naïve.

❀

With fans, boundaries are everything! While a drunken conversation might be a bit awkward, unfortunately, it is part of the job. However, that does not mean that you are required to put up with harassment of any kind. If things are getting inappropriate, you have a few options. Ask the person to stop (if you feel safe doing so). Tell a friend, another performer, or the bar staff. Tell security. If nothing is being done and you are feeling unsafe, you have no obligation to step foot outside of the dressing room. Usually it does not escalate to that point, but remember, your safety always comes first.

❀

If someone approaches you disrespectfully, drunk and belligerent, you notify security and have them escorted out. Many bars do not tolerate discrimination or acts of hatefulness towards entertainers.

❀

There is always the chance of a heckler, be it an audience member or another performer. I like to treat everyone like an adult, until they act like a child. I like to treat drunk hecklers like children. I give them a warning, embarrass them publicly, then have them removed if they cannot start acting like an adult. If a customer aggressively approaches me, I tell them directly how I feel. "Please do not touch me" if you feel uncomfortable is a professional response, if they do not listen; they need to be removed immediately.

❀

When doing shows you must be aware that there will always be a bad tomato in the garden. Reacting aggressively is exactly what they want. Do not do it. As best as you can, get away and report the person to security so they can ensure the other entertainers and you will be safe.

❀

Whenever someone is not drag friendly in a bar, or even when they try to approach me in the club to give a negative opinion, I always make sure to pay them no mind. Be safe, and keep your guard up. Including, having my friends and drag family around at the time of the altercation. I pay them no attention because haters exist. I do not let one word hinder my opinion of myself. Why would I let a complete stranger who does not even know me, affect my life in such a negative, dramatic way? I just do not. I keep the positivity flowing. Compliment them on their attire, or smile, and keep moving on.

❀

NEVER BE ALONE! In the bar if you are facing harassment, have them removed. I have found that if it is a harmless drunk heckling, learn to use it to your advantage. Become quick and sharp, generally shutting them down with a well-placed comical insult; NOT a direct personal insult. The majority of the audience is probably on your side and thinks the person is an asshole too. If you have them on your side, you are usually safe. When you leave the venue, ask an entourage to join you!

❀

Stick together, safety on numbers. If I see a customer getting worked up, I tell the bar staff right away, as well as all the other performers, and even any fans in attendance. The more eyes on the troublemaker, the better!

❀

I have been in a situation where I actually was hit onstage. I do not think you can ever be prepared for every situation, but we can love one another and hopefully love will be contagious.

❀

Security!

❀

Okay, so harassment as a whole is not welcome. I was brutally harassed to the point of almost suicide and recently, this year, found out that one of the NOH8 cofounders was bullying me secretly to the sources that were aggressive. So simply understand, if customer or individual is bullying you, it is because they're jealous of your look, success, or the fact that you can be what they can't.

❀

If you feel unsafe in an establishment, let someone know immediately. Know your way around the bar in case you need to get out quick. Be open with staff and management. If they want you in their bar, they need to ensure your safety and the safety of others.

If someone in the audience ever came up to me after I was offstage, and were out of line in any way, the bosses were there or the owners of the bar, and they were asked to leave or they would call the police. The places I worked did not go for any of that. They even had people in the parking lots making sure nothing happened outside.

Bars have security, but if they attack you, you have the right to defend yourself. Always be professional. Carry yourself professionally. Not everyone is going to like what you do. Whatever you do, handle situations professionally and calmly. Do not let some ignorant drunk detour you from doing what makes you happy.

Not everybody likes a female impersonator or a drag impersonator. Some people are afraid of them and intimidated because they do not understand it. They do not have any desire to be a drag impersonator, cross dresser, or impersonator. Everything comes back to mutual respect and kill them with kindness. Say, "I respect your opinion but you really do not know me. I am a nice person." That works a lot, catches them off guard. Of course, onstage I might handle that a little differently because I would actually use their energy as part of my act.

If someone heckled you, let them play along and let them see it does not bother you. A thick skin will make you more professional. Do not waste your time or energy on a Negative Nancy. As for them approaching you, if they give you an issue, politely say, "That is your opinion and you're entitled to it, but I do not have to stand here and listen. That is my right." Now, if it gets nasty, walk away. Do not be a tough guy or gal and ruin what you're working for. They are not worth it.

If there is someone harassing you after a show, let the bar owner know, and security, so that someone knows that you feel unsafe. If it continues, contact the authorities.

I never had a bad experience with members of our community and my choice to do drag. I have talked to people who do not like drag shows because a drag impersonator crossed the line, invaded their space. I showed these people that I would never do those things and engaging them in conversation to humanize drag impersonators is how I build trust with those people.

Oh boy! Hecklers are the worst! This is when you read them for filth. No one will stick up for you as much as you will and this is where the reading of each other as entertainers comes in handy. We sharpen each other's wits because we have to be tougher and smarter than our haters and hecklers. Most of the time the heckler will get embarrassed and leave or a bar staff member will remove them. Aggressive customers always happen, the point is not to escalate them because they really enjoy you and are being aggressive about that because they are drunk. I usually make a witty remark and say something along the effect of, "Oooo, I have to go to the ladies room, my manhood is calling," and they laugh and I make a quick escape. The nice thing about drunk customers is sometimes they tip really big because they do not know better, so it comes with the territory.

❀

Always keep it classy. Keep moving forward from them. If it gets too much to handle, you tell the bar. Always keep a distance and always surround yourself by people that make you feel comfortable.

❀

If there is someone in the bar who is being disruptive to the point where you are uncomfortable, alert the bar owner or manager. It is not up to you to control the bar crowd, and one aggressive, harassing customer can ruin the entire experience for everyone.

❀

Hecklers while I am onstage are ripped a new asshole verbally. I do standup comedy and come prepared with lots of insults that shut down a heckler quickly. I am 6'6 in stocking feet, 7' with hair and heels, so I am quite intimidating. I have never been approached or confronted offstage.

❀

If they are drunk, let them act the fool. Get the audience on your side as quickly as possible by pointing out he/she is ruining the show for everyone. Of course, this only works if you are good. If you are bad, maybe just side step out of the situation. Hecklers believe they are funnier than you are, so let them try. Pull them onstage, give them a mic, and watch them self-destruct before your very eyes. If someone is talking while I am speaking, I politely go up to them and say the following, "Sweetheart. Are you in show business? No? Then shut the fuck up!"

❀

Remain professional. I hope that the venue would protect the entertainer from physical harm.

❀

Just keep reminding yourself that art is subjective. If the heckler gets too out of hand, never hesitate to contact security.

❀

I absolutely do not deal with this kind of people. I have security escort them out of the bar.

❀

You must be careful. Sometimes you can joke around with the heckler and even pull them onstage and say, "You go entertain the crowd!" As for the aggressive customer, it is better to hold a smile, treat them with kindness, but be careful; they could have a knife or something. Have friends get security quick.

❀

Ideally, just diffuse the situation with something like, "you are welcome to your opinion" or "I am not bothering you so please have some decency." I hope that whatever venue you are at has some security, if not; they certainly have some sort of harassment policy. Even if you are not working for/at the bar, if someone is harassing you and will not leave you alone, find security or any staff person and let them know the situation. Defend yourself but do not do anything that could bring physical harm to yourself/others and do not do anything that can put you in bad light in the eyes of the venue/bar. If you cannot diffuse a situation, seek help.

❀

I just laugh it off, because you cannot please everyone and security should be there to diffuse the situation. If they approach you, try to be professional.

❀

When offstage surround yourself with people who want to be around you and love drag. Not everyone is into it, but if you come across someone who is rude, just ignore them and continue talking with someone you know nearby. Either they will go away or one of your friends will step in and show them the door

❀❀

If you are on the mic, like I am a lot, you will always get a heckler. That is when you have to decide which way to take the harassment. I personally go for broke and make them part of the show. I heckle back and try to break the ice. Sometimes it works and they back off. If not, I let them know I am happy they came out to support and ask them to be respectful of the entertainers. Afterwards they either leave, but more times than not, they smile and leave things alone. If you are lucky, they say thanks for F'ing around with them. Surprisingly I get that response a good bit.

❀

Just because one or more people do not like it, they do not have to be a part of it nor see it. Be strong for yourself and do not buy into people's negativity.

❀

It is not so much in the action but the reaction. We are professional and should conduct ourselves as such. If a person is aggressive, remove yourself. Do not feed or get into an altercation with them. Especially if they are drunk. They are not in a mindset to be rational with. Notify the owners or security and have them address the situation.

❀

Well, my first thought is, "Honey, if you are not into Drag, etc., why in the hell are you in a gay bar?" Second, I have dealt with my share of dumbfucks who have drunk their weight in Liquid Courage. Some fights, I have lost. Most, I have won.

❀

ALWAYS LET THE BAR MANAGER, SECURITY, OR SHOW DIRECTOR HANDLE IT. Try to get to a safe place away from a "bully" and notify the proper bar authority.

❁

I have learned it is best to maintain a sense of professionalism at ALL times, even when it is difficult. Therefore, I ignore hecklers. They are just looking for attention. Speaking as an alcoholic I can tell you first hand, verbal banter with someone who is intoxicated is pointless and a complete waste of time. You are there to entertain, pay attention to those audience members who are enjoying the show. As for dealing with an aggressive customer approaching them offstage, once again, I believe in professionalism at all times. Rather than take matters into your own hands, which could get you fired even if you feel justified, get security to handle the situation and have them escort the individual(s) out of the venue.

❁

Well I find that in this case, if you are able to - ignorance is bliss. Otherwise, a good quick quip to set your point and shut up the bastard sometimes helps - but remember if they were drunk, they most likely would not remember a damn thing anyway.

❁

To answer both questions, I walk away from such people. Their aim is to start trouble, and it serves no useful purpose to give them what they want.

❁

Want to be freaked out about your aggressive customers, read the fucking bovel by Todd Kachinski Kottmeier, "Turn Around Bright Eyes" about the serial killer going around killing drag queens about twenty years ago. Fuck!

❁

Be prepared to be able to keep the show moving along, using the heckler as a prop rather than a hurdle. The key is not to necessarily insult them personally, but to approach the situation where the audience can join in and you can keep the momentum without confrontation. When offstage, especially leaving, have a plan. Be safe. This not only applies to being in drag, but in general at a place where people can lose their inhibitions. I always have a lay of the establishment, have some sort of protection on me, and have sensible flats on.

❁❁

> "Nothing you wear onstage
> will be more spectacular
> than wearing confidence."
> Todd Kachinski Kottmeier

Chapter Nine

❀❀❀

How do they survive their own self-doubt?
Self-doubt: noun, lack of confidence in oneself and one's abilities.

Note: To maintain the integrity of this project, I did not edit most of the postings to allow the message sent in, to be in the actual words of the impersonator. I left them anonymous to allow the reader to understand them without pre-conceived bias.

❀

I am my own worst enemy. I am harder on myself than other people are on me. Remember to just be you and the best possible you that you can be. Be confident on the image and entertainment that you are providing and always maintain a level of positivity. Allow your confidence to exude you. As an impersonator, remember that you get the opportunity to play many different hats and others are often just stuck with one.

❀

Write a list of the things you like about yourself. Everyday come up with one, write it on a post-it, and place it on your bathroom mirror before you go to bed. That way every morning, you start the day on a positive note. Face your fears and love yourself. You are beautiful.

❀

Your mirror does not lie; see your flaws. Try to be better each time. Women and performers come in all shapes, sizes, and beauty. Most importantly, never compare yourself to anyone. Acceptance of one's self is important. I cannot really dance. I am not as beautiful as most. My personality and charm wins my crowd. My stage presentation is professional, funny, and captivating. My good points, out way my lack in other areas.

❀

Self-doubt happens all the time, some worse than others. If you feel down about your craft, do not be afraid to ask for help or advice from your friends or other performers. Those are the people who will be honest with you and not kick you when you are down

❦
If you love yourself, there is no self-doubt.
❦

Love yourself. Know that everyone starts somewhere. You will always be your own worst critic. Find something inside that makes you happy. If you are having doubts and you know wearing your favorite shirt gives you confidence, wear it. Doing you can never be wrong.

❦

Typically, this comes from lack of practice or low self-esteem. Practice, practice, practice, all we do is lip sync and shake our butts around. Practice it, not trying to be harsh, but if you are confident when rehearsing, you will kill it on stage! If you have low self-esteem, just know gays love big girls and bois. Gay people are typically very accepting of all types. If you're looking to lose a little weight just to feel better about yourself, practice will make you shed some sweat. Performing is not easy, honestly, in the least. You truly have to give it your all and want people to keep coming back to see you!

❦

Be yourself.

❦

This never really goes away, even after 6 years in my case. I do really weird, theatrical performances, including horror-drag. I worry that people would not "get" me... but then surprisingly, I had fans coming up to me or saying hi outside of shows. Just keep going. Another performer told me, "You really remind me of old school kings. People might not always get it, but you have to make them like it."

❦

There are always going to be times when you doubt yourself. Every single performer doubts themselves no matter what stage of the game they are in. It is a normal part of being an artist. It means that you care about your craft and want to make it better. Lean on your support system when you are doubting yourself. Most of all, remind yourself why you are doing this.

❦

A very dear friend had always told me, "you will always be nervous when you hit the stage, when you do not get nervous anymore, that is when you do not give your all on stage."

❦

Relax. Think about your closest friends and biggest supporters. Do you respect their opinions and beliefs? I imagine you do if they are close friends. Now what do they think of you? I imagine they care about you quite a bit and think you're pretty fantastic. Think of their encouraging words and how much you believe they would never steer you wrong. Then put on your favorite numbers while you are getting ready for your evening and start early to give yourself time to dance around and be silly between steps in your preparation process. Enjoy yourself.

We all doubt ourselves at some point or another. I do many, many times. You just have to find that reason as to why you like being a performer and constantly remind yourself of that. Surrounding yourself with positive, real people will help with that as well.

❊

Keep it going. You started for a reason. No one asked you to, or maybe they did. No one gave you permission. No one is funding you. No one is practicing your moves, dress, and makeup. No one is picking your music and style. No one is telling you how to be you, in drag or out of drag. Would you let them tell you what you could or could not do or how to do or not do it if you were not doing drag? Probably not.

❊

I know tons about this one. I get nervous even after doing this for 3 years. Do this for yourself. If you do something for the audience and they do not respond then tough shit on them. You go out and rock that number for you and as long as you are having fun that should be all that matters.

❊

Practice, practice, and practice some more until you know it in your sleep. It becomes like singing the ABC's. You no longer think about the performance, just having fun with it and the interaction of the audience. When you really know the number, the crowd will appreciate it and YOU. Do these EVERY time you hit the stage and your self-confidence will grow (but it takes WORK).

❊

I always struggle with self-doubt as a performer. Just continue to improve your skills as a performer; your self-confidence will grow with it.

❊

Remember that you are beautiful. You are strong and smart and you can practice a good contour and dancing but you are so much more than that. You are an impersonator, or a king. You are royalty.

❊

Confidence is the key to success.

❊

Always the toughest issue. Unless you have been instilled with a lifetime of support and validation leading to great self-confidence and appreciation, it is a challenge to generate it. Best I can suggest is small victories. Focus and become really good at one thing, (makeup, costuming, movement, dance, banter) and build on each small success, the greatest at anything have failed more times than most have even tried.

❊

At the end of the day, no matter if it is family, neighbors, lovers, dates, friends, coworkers, or drunk assholes, we are our own worst enemy. The worst comments that have ever been made to me were from myself. You cannot let the negative win. You have to do it because you love it. It takes time to build confidence.

❈

Drag is an expression art. There is no perfect how-to manual on how to do things right. Channel that self-doubt into something constructive. No one is confident 100% of the time, I am surprised myself sometime by the self-doubt that comes from entertainers who I consider to be extremely accomplished and well known in the community. Do not let self-doubt stop you, put it in its place, and let it motivate you. Your worst critic will always be yourself, and that is okay so long as you do not let it cripple you.

❈

Everyone has times when they feel like they are not good enough. We all do. The best thing to do is remember your best qualities and try to focus on your strengths. Work on weaknesses offstage and know that even the big shots have bad days.

❈

Performing is what I love, what keeps me sane. I push through all of the crap because I get to do what I love.

❈

This is something I still struggle with, even after being reassured by my partner, my friends, colleagues, show directors, etc. I generally do not talk about how much I doubt myself, because I do not want to come across as insecure. I take the negative feelings and try to figure out what does not feel right, why does not it feel right, and change it in the future. My partner always tells me, "Get out of your head." They are right. Just be there and enjoy yourself. That is why we do this. It is supposed to be fun.

❈

It is ok, and completely normal, to be nervous. Keep in mind; you are your own worst critic. We have all done things on stage that look weird. The only person who will put any thought into it after you get off stage is you. Take chances! It is better to put on a show - even if you are afraid that it would not look right - then to do nothing for fear of making a mistake. Every time you step on a stage, it is an opportunity to try new things and improve your drag.

❈

Everyone always goes through phases of self-doubt no matter how long they have been doing this, whether it is a look, or performance, or even if they feel they just cannot do it. They just need to remember that if they love entertaining then nothing can stop them! Never be afraid to try new things to grow as an entertainer! Just remember there is a fine line between being confident and conceited, so stay humble, but stay strong and beautiful!

❈

We all go through it. Sometimes we need to step back and look at what we have accomplished. Look at where you want to go and take a break from drag to find our confidence again.

❀

Self-doubt cannot only be something you survive, but it can be an asset. Without self-doubt, you may not have the drive to look at yourself as critically as everyone else is going to look at you. Do not let self-doubt cripple you, instead work hard to perfect the aspects of your character that need work. People with no self-doubt tend to throw the same tired attempts at Drag onto the stage over and over. You can do better than that!

❀

Know that all great performers/impersonators: all have had missteps and mishaps in their performances. Allow those mistakes to happen. You do not have to imitate any other performer. Create your own performance. You will be awesome, and does take time to build your fan base. However, your fans and supporters are out there.

❀

I think if an entertainer did not have self-doubt, they would not be motivated to do more for themselves. It is okay to doubt yourself from time to time, its normal. It is when you get cocky that you start truly failing. Always be humble and always thank your audience and the people you work with. Never get caught up in yourself.

❀

Sometimes in this industry, you lose the ability to remain confident. It is tough when there are so many unique and incredible individuals who also take part in this career. It is hard, but you have to keep believing. I always tell myself that I am worth it. That no matter what, I will always be just as unique as any other drag performer and I will always spread my name by kindness. It is about "loving yourself and knowing your self-worth is your biggest component."

❀

You have to remember to take drag for what it is. It is meant to be fun! If you are not having fun, do not do it. As cliché as it is, everyone started somewhere. You do not have to be the best, just be YOUR best. I lost my drive and motivation for a while because I did not think I was getting any better at drag, and got it back when I realized that it is okay not to be perfect. Just have fun!

❀

I did not think I could do it. I was older when I started, but it was always a love of mine. If you doubt yourself, do not be yourself; instead create a character for yourself. Remember, you can quit whenever you want and start whenever you want. It is Drag not brain surgery.

❀

Self-doubt is by far the biggest problem I face as a drag performer, it is an everyday struggle. I have learned that my doubt does come from within. I was taught to believe that drag is just wrong. I must constantly remind myself that I am perfect just the way I am. Drag brings a lot of joy and inspiration to people that may really need it.

❀

Not everyone is great at everything. That is why we need all types to make the world go around. That person may never know when they truly make a difference.

❀

Self-confidence comes with knowing one's self, it does not happen overnight, but eventually! Be the best person you can be! Do good, be good, wish well for others! Being true and genuine brings greatness!

❀

It took a while to get past the belief I was not good enough. Friends taught me to hold my head high because regardless of what you feel, someone sees something different, and when you find that someone, or those friends, that self-doubt goes away.

❀

Go back to the roots of your performer self. Why did you start? What inspired you? When I go back to the start of myself, I get rejuvenated and refreshed. To see the progress I have made reaffirms my love and confidence in the art form.

❀

Go out there leaving everything out on the stage, if you doubt yourself, it will be visible to the crowd. I personally have one drink before I perform if I am nervous, not to get drunk or whatever, but just to help me relax if I am nervous, just limit the alcohol. I have seen girls get messy doing this.

❀

That is something they need to do within themselves and no one can do it for them. It can be a very hard thing to do but I will say that I have seen some people self-medicate themselves in many different ways to make them feel better about themselves while doing shows, and I can tell you right now, that is not the answer and does not work. It takes inner strength to have confidence in yourself and if you have it then other people will also see you have it and they will also have confidence in you, but you have to have it in yourself first and it will show that you have it, because it will show in your performance.

❀

I tell myself every time I go out to a show, new job, or whatever, "I have been doing this for over 50 years." It boosts my confidence and makes me feel good. Try it.

❀

Everyone has self-doubt to begin with. You just have to get out there and give it your all. All that matters is that you are having fun. So have fun with it! Drag is something that is there for you to have a release from the real world. You get to put on makeup and a wig becoming someone else for the night. Some of the impersonators today push pageants too much. It is not about that. It is about entertaining a crowd and having fun.

❀

There are always times in your life you are going to have self-doubt. I have experienced it and at the end of the day, there was no cause for it. It happens, you just got to pick yourself up and move on. That is my motto, move on, move on, move on. One example was a few years ago due to health reasons, I could no longer wear pumps. It bothered me and still does that I have to wear flat shoes. Somebody said to me if they have to look at your feet, it means you have no talent. I try not to let it bother me.

❀

Look in the mirror and say, "I am handsome or pretty," and repeat it. Remember you are great and never have doubt. Everyone has it, but it's up to you to find what makes you happy. Live, laugh, love, and remember Carpe Deim (seize the day); be happy. You will get through it.

❀

If you're doubting yourself, watch your videos. If you feel you should have done something better, practice. My drag dad always says, "Proper preparation prevents poor performance." Make sure you are prepared and you know your words. Once you get on the stage you see people moving to your song and many people will dance and sing with you and just participate, your confidence goes up. In order to feel confident though, you must always be prepared.

❀

Being a larger sized impersonator is hard. I have doubted myself since I became an entertainer. My already being self-conscious about my size and not being able to dance and move around like the smaller guys. The binding when you have huge breasts. I have learned from this that no two people are alike. You are your greatest fan. No matter what happens, always love yourself and what you believe in. It is easier said than done, but do not ever give upon yourself and art form. Always remain positive in your thoughts and you will do great things.

❀

Practice self-care frequently- on stage and off! We all have days when we doubt ourselves, but we can counteract that by putting in place a series of healthy behaviors that remind us of who we are and of what we are capable of. I choose kindness. If someone causes me to feel badly about myself, I turn around and do something nice for someone else - it is really helpful to be kind to strangers! That tends to soothe my self-doubt and reassure myself that I am just having a challenging day. I already turned it around by being kind to someone else. If all else fails, remember, the best thing about today is tomorrow!

❀

There will be days that we all have lack of confidence in ourselves but we have to look at our weakness so that we can be stronger and learn to do better for our own worth.

❀

The key to confidence is doing and receiving rewards. If you have fans who are your friends at a show, they will still be your friends afterwards, and no matter what you do, they will support you. That support creates confidence because those friends will give you positive feedback and the more you do it the easier it will become.

❀

Drag is an evolution in your character and confidence. The foundation of drag should come from owning who/what your character's vision is. I feel a strong sense of purpose will provide confidence and lead to success in this industry. Here is a simple way to practice a daily self-affirmation. Look in the mirror every morning and ask yourself, "Who Am I?" Answer with a strong, confident and caring tone (it's just you and the mirror) who you want to be (if you're not sure yet, who you are). I ask myself every morning. It changes from day to day, but the base stays the same. "I am a colorful, creative, and unique genderqueer individual; serving raunchy fierceness since 1997! I am grateful today to spread the GLAM."

❀

At some point, you will question yourself, "Why you are doing this?" It happens to all of us and it is usually around the 1-2 year mark. If you need to take a break, do it, refrain from making public announcements or venting online. You do not want to look wishy washy if someone gives you a gig you would really enjoy doing but you said you were taking a break. I keep myself invested by buying new drag, learning a skill like sewing, hair, and always changing up the way I paint my face. This keeps it interesting for me and is constantly pushing me for bigger goals. Drag is about being Confident and those who are not, struggle major on stage.

❀

You can only change you. If there is something you don't like, change it. NEVER GIVE UP. Everyone starts from the bottom. If female illusion is truly a passion, you will do anything to overcome not feeling good enough.

❀

My self-doubt and confidence has been shot down many times. I have told myself that my entertaining is an art, a gift. I have told myself, I am as good as I want to be. Always have confidence within yourself, that is when you will find the confidence in who you are.

❀

Everyone doubts themselves sometimes. Ask for help, ask for feedback, be willing to learn and grow. Push boundaries; try something new.

❀

Work hard and ask for help, once I found a nice, experienced, successful performer. Even after thirty years as a drag impersonator, I pay for makeup lessons and practice, practice, practice. I will pay a performance arts dance company to choreograph my numbers. I am always open to helpful criticism and willing to learn and grow.

❀

Rinse and repeat. If you are unsure about makeup, do it over and over, and over, and over, and over, until you are. If you are unsure about performing, do the same fucking thing. You would not get over anything just thinking about it. You need to do it. Self-doubt is always there, if you ever feel it go away... Watch a YouTube of yourself with a quickness, because you need to see you are not as good as you thought you were. Use the feelings of self-doubt to make your performance stronger, your outfits cuter, and your attitude better. Having confidence and being proud of a performance is one thing, but losing fear or self-doubt completely makes you complacent and eventually boring as fuck to watch.

❀

Talk with a personality that is both open and friendly in sharing their confidence in a positive manner.

❀

Practice, practice, practice. 18 years in, I still have self-doubt. It's normal, and applied correctly, it can drive you to be amazing.

❀

You have to look yourself in the mirror and realize that you are beautiful and talented. You HAVE to love yourself or this industry will eat you alive!

❀

We all have self-doubt no matter what. Remember, drag is for fun. Even the top drag impersonators still carry doubt. You must have confidence in yourself. When you do, the audience will see it and the tips will role in. If you go out there scared, well, everyone will turn and walk away.

❀

All artists, all people in fact, have to deal with self-doubt at some point. Some more than others but everyone deals with it to some degree at various points during our lives. Anyone who tells you they have always known what they wanted to be and have never had a doubt in their mid is kidding themselves. Self-doubt is not necessarily a bad thing, it is simply our rational minds trying to weigh whether the effort being put in to a goal is actually going to yield a beneficial result or not. It is how one deals with self-doubt that is important. Again, ask yourself why you are doing drag. Do you get creative fulfillment from drag? Is drag financially beneficial? Do you have friends, colleagues in the drag community and fans that you enjoy working with/entertaining? MOST IMPORTANTLY, do you have fun? If you are having fun and are enjoying success in drag then remind yourself that we all experience doubt and those thoughts are neither bad nor good. Put those thoughts from your mind. If, however, you are working hard at drag and not improving and not getting financial benefit, and people are not supportive, and, most importantly, if you are not having fun... then you are probably justified in your self-doubt. Drag is nothing more than a shit-ton of hard work if you are not having fun doing it. A healthy amount of self-doubt never hurt anybody; deal with it rationally.

❀

You're going to have a little doubt. We are human and a lot of times the audience will give you the encouragement from the reaction they give. It could be negative or positive, but remember, this is just an interpretation, and will be just to make you handle the good and bad, because it will give you thick skin. You need that to be successful in drag.

❀

Do not expect to be a star when you hit the stage. It takes years of practice, rehearsals, and talent shows to get to a place where you are known and respected. Have confidence that you are doing the best you can and seek out advice from others who have been in the business, and never let the drama and backstabbing get you down. Practice, practice, practice, and video yourself, and watch back to see where you can improve, and watch videos of other performers, both drag and professional performers, and take a little here and a little there until you create your persona.

❀

I was placed in a very awkward situation very early in my career. This club I worked in had an annual event called the "Flawless Awards" and my first year I got "Least Promising Newcomer" and was told I could only do comedy drag (at the time I was only doing a character impersonation of Bette Midler) and that I would NEVER be pretty enough to do "Glamour" drag. Well, in my case it ignited a fire inside me, making me want to show them. I persisted and went above and beyond all of their "Prophecies." Sometimes you just have to set your mind to your goals and do your homework, work hard and you will get there.

❀

If you are lucky enough to find a seasoned mentor then learn all you can. My mentor gave me great advice. "Choose music that you connect with and that the audience can believe. If they can see that you are enjoying yourself and truly feel the music, you can't miss." Quote by Lady Ace VonCosta (She may not remember but I do.)

❀

Talk to people whom love and care about you. My family has helped me a great deal in my self-doubt and not wanting to give up on what I enjoy doing.

❀

Self-doubt is something that we all face eventually in our lives. Honey, if I would have taken what Auntie Carma told me all those years ago to heart, I would have never met some of the most amazing people I have ever known or blossomed the way I have as an Entertainer.

❀

Doubting yourself will show in your performances... practice, practice, practice in your home if you feel insecure. Gather a small group of close friends and perform in your living room for them, and let them tell you how you did. Take constructive criticism and apply it!

❦

Many performers feel this way, including myself to this very day. My view on it is that we only fail when we refuse to try, and no matter how nervous an entertainer is, once they hit the stage, they should never let 'em see you sweat (meaning the audience). If you have to throw up before you go on, and after you come off, that is fine, but while you are actually on the stage, you got to fake it till you make it. Get out there and do the very best you are capable of and own it.

❦

The great thing about drag is that we all have our own abilities. If you know yours, then you are a step ahead of the game. The trick is to turn it into something that is entertaining. Enhance those moneymakers baby! If you doubt yourself, it will only be a matter of time before you sabotage yourself and ruin yourself from performing.

❦

I always do my best when performing, despite a disability. That is all I CAN do. I ask nothing less of myself than that.

❦

It can be a hard decision. I advise people in my professional life to get a piece of paper and draw a line down the middle, listing the pros and cons of a certain decision. In this case, it would be what makes being a performer so special in your life and how much would not performing negatively affect it. I am always thankful for the existence of drag. I went for years trying to find an avenue to creatively express myself, but until I was able to take on an alternative persona, I always felt trapped by my day-to-day shortcomings. Honestly, you may decide it is not the thing for you and the cons outweigh the pros, but that will have to be your decision and yours alone.

❦❦

> "People feeling lost never truly see
> the massive amount of people supporting them.
> This is me, telling you, I am here. I care; we care."
> Todd Kachinski Kottmeier

Chapter Ten

❋❋❋

What words can you share overall to give the reader encouragement?

Note: To maintain the integrity of this project, I did not edit most of the postings to allow the message sent in, to be in the actual words of the impersonator. I left them anonymous to allow the reader to understand them without pre-conceived bias.

❋

My GAYz always thought for some reason I was cheating when it came to altering my body too compete and perform. I was ALWAYS feminine and had feminine features. I strive to exude and be like the transgender girls competing such as Miss Continental. I sometimes put my award winning talent on hold because not many had both talent and beauty. I was determined. Looking back, I probably would not have gone as far with silicone injections, for its proven to be deadly. I urge up and coming impersonators to stick with their talent. Beauty will eventually shine through!

❋

Follow your passion and make sure you are giving the best version of you possible. Be proud of who you are and always allow yourself the opportunity to grow...inside and out. Involve others and surround yourself with love and support and close out the negative surroundings that may hold you back or make you feel self-doubt.

❋

A lot of the time, if other performers are giving you a hard time, it is because they perceive you as a threat in the future instead of an ally. Do NOT back down but ask if you can help. Watch EVERYTHING they do and see if their way is better or not. Be a sponge and NEVER give up. If you have a TRUE passion for the craft, you WILL persevere!

❋

Do not ever be afraid to be new to the game; that is any game, really. If you are new, ask questions. Play with your style to learn about yourself as a performer and a human being. Even when you are way down the line, and you have been doing it for years, do not be afraid to be new. There is nothing worse than going stale to yourself, and if that means completely revamping yourself to fit what YOU want better, than so be it... and always, always, always remember that "impersonator" or "king" is there for a reason. You are royalty. You are fabulous, you sparkle, and you are a good person, no matter what anyone else tells you.

❊

Open and honest with self and others. No shame, guilt, or apologies for being you. Realize shortcomings, embrace them, improve them, but do not dwell on them. Love yourself completely. Good, bad, and different.

❊

As cliché as it is, "Those who matter, do not mind. Those who mind, do not matter" I have lived by this for some time now and it always helps me out. There is always going to be that ONE person that will not like you no matter what you do. Take that and RUN WITH IT! Apparently there is something that person is jealous of about you. That is life babes!

❊

Hunny, you are a beautiful individual and if you have the guts to do drag, strut that catwalk with that diva attitude.

❊

If you cannot love yourself, no one else can, either.

❊

I know you will do it justice no matter how you spin it. I would rather deal with words rather than the beatings I used to get from kids as an overweight, white child in a prominently black neighborhood. Anyway, you get through it.

❊

Give your best performance every night! Some will land great, some will not. It is all about your style and what you are comfortable doing. Do not try to be someone you are not. Be who you want to be, and just have fun. Performing should be fun, you should enjoy doing it. So do what you enjoy and your audience will love it!

❊

Honesty, Unity, and being loyal.

❊

Be original. Think about who and what you want to be and hold onto that. Breathe life into it. Believe in it.

❊

Remember why you do this, it makes you happy and makes others happy. Take pictures and record your progress, this was something that kept inspiring me to go on. Don't be afraid to try new things. Don't be afraid to ask other performers for advice. Though some may not be open to it, there are more performers who want to see you do well and are open to giving advice. Always remain humble and open for critiques. A bad attitude can ruin a pretty face or a good performance. Most of all,

HAVE FUN! Performing is supposed to be fun above all else. You also never know whose day you are going to change with your craft so SMILE and always be friendly.

❀

Be true to yourself first and then to your family and friends.

❀

The only person that has to like you is you. You are the one that has to live with yourself. Unless they are feeding you, financing you, or fucking you, then your life is not anybody else's business.

❀

Patience and persistence are very powerful tools!

❀

Do you. No one else is going to do you. No one else can Most people do not even want to do themselves. Do you want to be famous one day because of someone else's molding or your own? In the end, nothing matters because we all end up in the same place. You might as well do what you love for you while you are here.

❀

Keep your head up. Do not let anyone tell you who you are or what you should be. Oh yea and pageants ARE NOT the end all be all to drag. Do not let anyone tell you that you are not going to be someone without a title; and RuPaul's drag race is not how real drag works!

❀

Learn to love with all your heart and accept the lovable sides of others. For anyone can love a rose, but only a great few can learn to love the thorns.

❀

Place your own self-worth high. NEVER let anyone take away from that value.

❀

Just do you. Do not ever be afraid to ask for help. There are a lot of groups on facebook that are more than willing to help or give advice; all you gotta do is ask.

❀

Never let anyone determine your self-worth!

❀

In the business of DRAG, there are many obstacles and hurdles. When you make the decision to become a performer, you have to take into account that you will not always come across people who are in your corner. There are many times that this can be a cutthroat business. YOU will win and LOSE. YOU will entertain some and you will make some enemies, but you must never let it deter you from your goal. DO NOT spend a lot of time worrying about your mistakes or what you could have done differently. LEARN from them. Ask entertainers who have been in the business awhile what you can do differently. LEARN from them. Do not be discouraged! Remember we all started somewhere and we all have been through the ups and downs. Ultimately, YOU are doing what you love to do and at the end of the night if you are happy with your performance, then that is all that really matters. Stay positive even in the face of adversity. DO NOT be afraid to try new things, new characters, eventually you will find your place in this business

❀

Be you. Love what you do. If someone is giving constructive criticism, listen to it. If someone is just being hateful, nod and smile. Do not blink either. It will freak them out. Be the performer you want to be and for God's sake!

❀

I cannot think of anything more challenging and satisfying than making the choice to become a male lead/entertainer. Always, always, always remember your community. Support them graciously and they will support you. Remember to have fun, it will show in your performance and that is a quality that can take a good performance and make it great.

❀

No matter what anyone says, do not give up. Not everyone will understand or be nice but you are valid and you are not alone. Get on that stage and shine in your own way and you will enjoy yourself. It's not always about crowns and winning, do not forget to have fun.

❀

Do what you love, hone your craft and prove every person who ever gave you shit or was cruel to you wrong. Learn to love yourself just as you are and spread that love to everyone you work with and that will change the world.

❀

No matter how good you may be, you can always improve. If people cannot be respectful, they are not worth your time.

❀

Never lose sight of who you are as a person and as a performer. Both identities are so important. Be true to yourself, even if you are met with resistance. Be genuine. Watch and learn. There is so much knowledge and skill in the individuals around you. Experience is one of the most valuable things. Learn from those who have been doing this far longer than you. Be confident in yourself, but stay humble. You are never done learning and the moment that you get cocky is the moment you start losing booking. No one wants to work with a snobby entitled performer.

❀

Love what you do and do what you love! Always help and not hurt! Stay humble and appreciate the blessings that are given to you! Words only have power if you give it to them! There is a fine line between being confident and conceited!

❀

Be nice to people, and they will be nice to you. Do not accept less than your best and the best of other people. Never tolerate intolerance.

❀

Every Drag character is on a journey, constant evolution, and every artist started somewhere. Although you may not feel 100% happy about where you are at any given moment, you CANNOT let your fears keep you from putting yourself out there. Make strong choices and follow your heart. Being afraid of where you are can never get you where you are going.

❀

Be who you are! You are unique and special because there is no one like you. Do not let anyone's words beat you down because those are just words. You are your own form of art; do not ever let anyone take that away from you.

❀

If I can say anything, it would be that you are worth it. You can be anything in this life that you have ever dreamed of. Just because someone else does not see it, does not mean that it does not exist. Your dreams are reality only if you make them. Work hard, be unique, and never change the person you are to make someone else happy. Do not fall into stereotypes, and do not turn your life into negativity. I believe in you, I am always here for you, and you should believe in you. It is a tough life, but if it is your dream, then go get it, baby!

❀

Keep your chin up. You never know how far you will go if you do not keep trying.

❀

Never take Drag too seriously. You are doing it to entertain people. If you are not having any fun, neither will the audience. You are never too old to start, and be an ambassador for your community, not an entitled little fake popstar!

❀

Be true to yourself always and forever! Try to educate those around you rather than persuade them into seeing your side. Most of all have fun, if you are confident and having fun people around you will do the same

❀

Trust yourself, grow, and love one another.

❀

Strive to make yourself happy, life will unfold, as it should. Find your inner peace and share it. Try not to judge anyone, accept all for who they are. Embrace your strengths and accept your weaknesses. No one person is, or ever will be perfect. You are your own destiny!

❀

Mission statement for National Do Not H8 Pageantry   "To recognize and celebrate each individual's differences through our message of one voice, one song, one dance, will make a change."

❀

Be true to yourself, follow your dreams. I grew up in the drag community when there were strong mentors; find a mentor who is willing to help you. There will always be bullies, but really what they think about you, is none of your business.

❀

We all know doing what we do is not easy; sometimes it sucks. There is always someone that understands what you are going through. Know your support group, support yourself by positive influences and most importantly... HAVE FUN!

❀

Being a part of any type of entertainment opens you up to immense amounts of criticism, which leaves you very vulnerable. The best advice I can give anyone who is struggling with drag haters (other performers or audience members) and self-doubt is remember why you perform. You are an entertainer and you do it because you love to entertain. The one thing you need to hold in the back of your head is, if you have someone who does not appreciate you as a performer, they are outnumbered by people who do. The most humbling piece of advice I have ever received is, "You are only as good as someone-else's opinion." Some people will love you, some people would not, it is a fact "that you cannot please everybody" and you will make yourself miserable trying to do so. At the end of the day, perform for you and never stop evolving because when you are on stage you are sharing yourself and everything you are worth as an entertainer with many people, and remember that even if you have a heckler, it's only one person and the majority of the audience enjoys the show.

❀

First and foremost, be true to yourself. Always, no matter, always treat the other performers with respect. Do not let anyone allow you to feel they are better than you. Do not take any bullying from anyone no matter who they are, stand up and be strong. Always be honest to who and what you are.

❀

Just be true to yourself. Drag is about having fun, entertaining the crowd. Do not get discouraged by the RuPaul crowd. That is only television propaganda and not the real world! Have fun with it! That is what drag is all about! Have fun! Drag is a profession where you are always learning. If someone tells you they know it all, they do not! Learn from impersonators with experience but never lose yourself!

❀

If being an impersonator, whatever you want to be, just do it. In your heart, you can live it. It is just a little idea that you want to give it a try go for it. I have entertained for 41 years. I still love what I do. Remember the important person here is you.

❀

Stay true to yourself. Anything worth it in life, you get from hard work, sacrifice, dedication, time, and patience. Remember this is a craft, an art form. It always should be fun! If not, find out why. The biggest lesson I was once told is, "the day you stop learning, growing, evolving, is the day you should hang it up." There is always room to improve and be better. If you do not know, ask someone! I always have your back. Good Luck!

❊

Just remember why you started doing drag. Keep your head up and always be prepared. Never feel like you cannot ask someone for advice and help. This is about coming together and about sisterhood and brotherhood.

❊

Please remember three things: you are lovable, you are valuable, and you are important. Do not let anyone tell you any different, and someday, you will believe those things. I know I do.

❊

Always believe in yourself even if no one else does. Remain positive and humble no matter how far you make it. Even when you feel like you cannot go on or not good enough. You are the greatest entertainer to yourself even though things may get tough. There is a dream, so live it and love it. When others offer encouragement and try to mentor you, listen. It does not hurt to hear advice.

❊

When we feel that we lack power, we often feel sad, depressed, harassed, and unimportant. Know that the power to achieve, to breathe, and to grow resides inside yourself. Drag is about creating art and community that supports social and intersectional justice. Know that you can unearth from within yourself the power to be part of this movement. Knowing yourself is key. Any perceived failure on your part is nothing more than a way to grow into the understanding, open, and wonderful artist who you are.

❊

There will be good days and there will be bad ones, too...but always remember to be true to yourself and your craft. No one can be a better you than you. Do not let anyone or even yourself feel like you are not worthy. We all have our reasons for going into the entertaining business so remember that, and then retire whenever you are ready on your own terms.

❊

Whether you just want to do it once or you want to make a career out of drag, success does not happen overnight. Everyone who is someone in this community has worked hard and honed in on their craft. I suggest finding something that makes you different from others. Embrace what type of performer you are and never give up.

❊

The best advice I can give anyone who is reading this book is a quote that I have heard recently, "A lion does not concern himself with the opinion of sheep."

❊

Drag is life changing. The art, the general community, the experience is an adrenaline rush. It is not for the faint of heart, but if you believe in yourself, develop your character, listen to those who came before you and constantly push yourself, you will have a blast. If you are doing this to make money, you are in the wrong profession.

❦

Stay true to you. Do not conform to anyone else's standards; otherwise, you will never be happy. Keep moving because you can only go up. As RuPaul has said, which I live by, "What people say about you is none of your business."

❦

I just want to say that loving yourself is the key to life. You do not live for others, and stay true to yourself and who you really are deep down inside.

❦

People will always trash talk. Not everyone will be okay with what you do. The way that you handle the haters will say more about who you are as a person and an entertainer than what the haters are saying. Keep learning, keep growing. Try new things. Experiment. Rise above the trash talk and those who seek to bring you down. There will always be the occasional rough patch, but you will get through it and you will be stronger for it.

❦

Just do you and be willing to learn and grow. Work hard and always give 100% even if there are only two people in the audience. Always be on time and call if you have to cancel. Always return kindness when given negativity. By agreeing with whatever they say, satisfies their ego. Always remember. What they say about you is truly a mirror of what they think and feel about themselves.

❦

You will always be your worst enemy and harshest critic. When you receive a compliment, appreciate it. Do not dismiss it, believe it, even if only for a few moments. You will become what you want to be, and that might not be what people like, it is what you like. For fuck's sake, invest in professional dance tights! Drugstore Pantyhose have no place on a man. If I see another girl with the control top of her Pantyhose exposed on her hips, OMG! They are not cheap, but last longer. I cannot tell you how many pairs I have forcefully given to little Latin boys in drag!

❦

Be yourself and love what you do even if no one else does.

❦

You are a gift. What we do brings smiles and laughter to people. Never give up.

❦

For me it is all about just being me. What you see is what you get. I am not caught up in the drama associated with this industry. I am a lady and therefore do not lower myself to other's level. There will always be someone putting you down or belittling you. Let them talk; they just make themselves look bad.

❦

You must have confidence in you. Drag is not cheap, but it's fun. Remember we are just men in a dress and wig to make someone's day brighter and send them home with a smile. So remember to always be humble and thank the audience. Never think you are better than everyone else is.

❀

Remember that drag should be fun! If you are not having fun you are wasting your time. Other people's opinions should have no bearing on something you love to do. If you work hard and have fun doing it most people will recognize and appreciate that and the ones that do not are insignificant and probably in the minority. Do not let those doubters bring you down to their level; show them love; lead by example, and they will rise to your level. We are never going to win-over everyone and you just have to let those people go from your thoughts and life. Finally, I think it is most important to distinguish between bullying and constructive criticism. Those impersonators that you know, are close to, you look-up-to, and trust, may deal you some harsh criticisms, but it is only because they love you and want to see you do well. Reading has always been an integral aspect of the drag community and it is usually not a bad thing. More experienced impersonators especially, have experienced the highest of highs and the lowest of lows and they would rather you hear it from them before outsiders with opinions, try to tear you to shreds. That having been said, you are an individual and you do not need to take all criticisms to heart (always listen) but you do not need to act on every criticism simply because it comes from someone you respect. Work hard, you do you, and have FUN!

❀

Be yourself and true to your beliefs. Always look, listen, and learn. You can learn from anyone, new or old to drag. Take what you learn and apply it to your vision. Never let people knock you down. Stand on your own feet. Practice your routine, wear pads and nails. Walk around in mall clothes; perform in costumes, not your mom's clothes. Costumes are something you would not wear to Walmart, unless it's a funny skit, then wear whatever fits the character.

❀

If you are doing drag because you feel you want to entertain people and have a talent or you are willing to take the time to learn routines and rehearse until your feel ache, then you should do well. If you have either a talent for making your own clothes and are proficient in your makeup and hair skills, you will do well. If you just want to be the center of attention and get up on stage and lip sync to your favorite performer, then stay at home. Do it in front of the mirror or for friends, the drag life is not for you. In all, it is a long and hard road and expensive with little return on investment. It is a calling and you must love it more than anything else you want to do in life.

❀

Remember one thing; your opinion of yourself is the only one that is of importance. Do not give this power to anyone that is not supportive or helpful of your art. Do not try to be anyone else but yourself. You are the only you. Watch, learn, borrow, and create your own persona. This will take you farther than just being a poor copy of another's concept. Your beauty and talent are strictly your own. Build your stage persona, and then go for it!

❀

Never belittle yourself or your creative self to make others accept or like you. You are one if a kind.

❀

Be yourself, do what makes you happy and there will always be people that will not like you but you are the only one that can choose what you want to hear, do not listen to people with a lot of hate towards you, they do not define you. Only you can define you and enjoy life.

❀

Being an impersonator, doing drag, and being an entertainer is all about having fun, showing the world your creativity and artistry, just remember that, and make sure you are doing it for the right reason. Make sure you know what you are doing, and make sure you know why you are doing it! Just remember: whatever you do, give it your all and all will be given back. The crowd knows when you put out your best and when your heart is in it, and if you can touch one person's life or make someone else feel a little better about themselves, and then your job is done. Because at the end of the day that is what we're here for, to entertain, to make people smile, and maybe, just for one second, to help people forget about the worries and just live life to the fullest

❀

You must be your biggest fan and remember why it is that you perform. Not everyone will like what you do, but as long as you the best of your ability, you will be respected. Always stay professional and remember this is an art.

❀

I could quote all sorts of people here, but I believe I will stick with a quote from My Aunt Cecilia: "The time has come to shed ourselves of the guilt, shame, and darkness of our lives, and to instead walk with our heads held high in the sunshine and love."

❀❀

Now, if this book brought you any comfort, pass it on.
❀❀
Better yet, get them their own copy!
DRAG411.com

Ten Black Books

Ten Black Books

Book 1   DRAG411's
"DRAG Bully, A Survivor's Guide"

The Largest Bullying Project in LGBT History for Struggling Entertainers. Advice from over a hundred male, female, and androgynous impersonators around the world to help entertainers struggling with their family, peers, relationships, neighbors, regular jobs, venues, and successfully overcoming self-doubt. Best Selling author Todd Kachinski Kottmeier created DRAG411 to document the lives of male, female, and androgynous impersonator years ago. It is now the largest organization for impersonators on earth with over 7,000 entertainers in 32 countries. DRAG411 also operates The International Original, Official DRAG Memorial with almost a thousand names (2018). This is his 25th book, 20th World Record, and 12th book on this subject. Thousands of invitations to contribute were send out. This book contains the best of their responses, in their own words, to you.

Book 2 DRAG411's **"Original DRAG Handbook"**

Over 155 female impersonators (and 1 male impersonator) from around the world share over a thousand insightful comments in the first handbook created of this art form.

Commentary shared with Todd Kachinski Kottmeier included the following contributors of The Original, DRAG Handbook to include Ada Buffet, Adora , Adrian Leigh, Afeelya Bunz, Alisa Summers, Alanna Divine, Alexis De La Mer, Alexis Mateo, Alex Serpa, Allure, Amanda Bone, Amanda Love, Amy DeMilo, Anastaia Fallon, Alexis De La Mer, Alexis Mateo, Angel gLamar, Angela Dodd, Anita Cox, April Fresh, Ashleigh Cooley, Aurora Sexton, Babette Schwartz, Bailey St. James, Barbra Herr, Barbra Seville, Beverly LaSalle, BJ Stephens, Blair Michaels, Brandon M. Caten, Brianna Lee, Brittany Moore, Brookyln Bisette, Bukkake Blaque London St. James, Cartier Paris, Cathy Craig, Champagne T. Bordeaux, Cherry Darling, Christina Paris, CoCo LaBelle, CoCo Montrese, CoCo St. James, Conundrum, Crystal Belle, Daniel Murphy, Danika Fierce, Daphne Ferraro, Dasha Nicole, Dee Gregory, Deva DaVyne, Diamond Dunhill, Diedra Windsor Walker, Dmentia Divinyl/Eva LaDeva, Echo Dazz, Esme Russell, Estelle Rivers, Eunyce Raye, Felica Fox, Felina Cashmere, Geraldine Queen Cabaret, Ginger Minj, Glitz Glam, Gilda Golden, Horchata, Ima Twat, Ineeda Twat, Jade Daniels, Jade Jolie, Jade Shanell, Jade Sotomayo, Jaeda Fuentes, Jami Micheals, Jay Santana, Jeffrey Powell, Jenna Chambers Tisdale, Jessica Jade, Jocelyn Summers, Jodie Holliday, Joey Brooks, Joshua Myers, J.P. Patrick, Juwanna Jackson, Kamden Wells, Katrina Starr, Kenny Braverman, Khrystal Leight, Kier Sarkesian, Kiki LaFlare Santangilo, Kitty D'Meaner, Kori Stevens, Krystal Amore Adonis, Lacey Lynn Taylors, Lady Clover Honey, Lady Sabrina, Lady TaJma Hall, Lakeisha Pryce, LeeAnna Love, Leigh Shannon, Lisa Carr, Lola Honey, Madisyn De La Mer, Makayla Rose Devine, Maxine Padlock (Maxi Pad), Melissa Morgan, Melody Mayheim, Michael Wilson, Mike Astermon-Glidden, Mis Sadistic, Miss Conception, Miss Gigi, Mr. Kenneth Blake, Misty Eyez, Monique Michaels, Myah Monroe, Mystique Summers, Nairobi V. D'Viante, Naomi D-Lish, Naomi Wynters, Nicole Paige Brooks, Nikki Dynamite, Nova Starr, Ororo, Patrica Grand, Patricia Knight, Patrica Mason, Pandora DeStrange, Penelope Reigns, Polly

FunkChanel, Phiore Star Liemont, Purrzsa Kyttyn, Pussy LeHoot, Raquel Payne, Rhyana Vorhman, Rickie Lee, Rusti Fawcett, Scarlett Fever, Selina Kyle, Shae Shae LaReese, Shealita Babay, Shugah Caine, Stephanie Roberts, Stephanie Stuart, Stormy Vain, Summer Breeze, Sybil Storm, Tabatha Lovall, Tatum Michelle, Teri Courtney, Tiffani Middlesexx, Timm McBride, Toni Davyne, TotiYanah Diamond,Trixie LaRue, Trixie Pleasures, Vegas Platinum, Venus D Lite, Vivika D'Angelo, Wendel Duppert and Wendy G. Kennedy.

Book 3: DRAG411's
"Crown Me! Winning Pageants"

Hundreds of invitations sent to the titleholders, pageant promoters, judges, and talent show hosts to share their insight on not only winning pageants and contests but also owning the stage every time they perform. Their topics included auxiliary steps to success needed for song selection, dancing, movement on stage, props, backup dancers, creating your own edge, personal interviews, steps to success for winning the talent category every time you step on stage, on stage questions, eveningwear, and creative costuming. They discussed in their own unedited words, wardrobe changes, makeup, hair, shoes, when is the time to compete, qualities needed for a judge, and the top misconceptions of contestants competing in the pageantry systems.

Commentary shared with Todd Kachinski Kottmeier included the following contributors of Crown Me! to include AJ Menendez, Amy Demilo, Anastacia Dupree, Anson Reign, Bob Taylor, Breonna Tenae, Brittany T Moore, Coco Montrese, Dana Douglas, Darryl Kent, Denise Russell, Dey Jzah Opulent, Freddy Prinze Charming, Gage Gatlyn, Jay Santana , Jayden Knight, Jennifer Foxx, Joey Jay, Kori Stevens, Mis Sadistic, Mykul Jay Valentine, Natasha Richards, Rico Taylor, Sam Hare, Stephanie Stuart, Taina T. Norell, Tiffani Middlesexx, Tori Taylor, Ty Nolan, Vinnie Marconi, and Vivika D'Angelo.

Book 4: DRAG411's
"DRAG King Guide"

Over 155 male impersonators around the world share over a thousand insightful comments in forty-one chapters.

Commentary shared with Todd Kachinski Kottmeier included the following contributors of The Official DRAG King and Male Impersonators Guide to include Aaron Phoenix, Abs Hart, Adam All, Adam DoEve, AJ Menendez, Alec Allnight, Alexander Cameron, Alik Muf, Andrew Citino, Anjie Swidergal, Anson Reign, Ashton The Adorable Lover, Atown, Ayden Layne, B J Armani, B J Bottoms, Bailey Saint James, Ben Doverr, Ben Eaten, Bootzy Edwards Collynz, Brandon KC Young-Taylor, Bruno Diaz, Cage Masters, Campbell Reid Andrews, Chance Wise, Chandler J Hart, Chasin Love, Cherry Tyler Manhattan, Chris Mandingo, Clark Kunt, Clint Torres, Cody Wellch Klondyke, Colin Grey, Corey James Caster, Coti Blayne, Crash Bandikok, Dakota Rain, Dante Diamond, Davion Summers, DeVery Bess, Devin G. Dame, Devon Ayers, Dionysus W Khaos, Diseal Tanks Roberts, D-Luv Saviyon, Dominic Demornay, Dominic Von Strap, D-Rex, Dylan Kane, E. M. Shaun, Eddie C. Broadway, Emilio, Erick LaRue, Flex Jonez, Freddy Prinze Charming, Gabe King, Gage Gatlyn, George De Micheal, Greyson Bolt, Gunner Gatlyn, Gus Magendor, Hawk Stuart, Harry Pi, Holden Michael, Howie Feltersnatch, Hurricane Savage, J Breezy St James, Jack E. Dickinson, Jack King, Jake Van Camp, Jamel Knight, Jenson C. Dean, Johnnie Blackheart, Jonah Godfather of DRAG, Jordan Allen, Jordan Reighn, Joshua K. Mann, Joshua Micheals, Juan Kerr, Julius M. SeizeHer, Jude Lawless, Justin Cider, Justin Luvan, Justin Sider, K'ne Cole, Kameo Dupree, Kenneth J. Squires, King Dante, King Ramsey, Jack Inman, Kody Sky, Koomah, Kristian Kyler, Kruz Mhee, Linda Hermann-Chasin, Luke Ateraz, Lyle Love-It, Macximus, Marcus Mayhem, Marty

Brown, Master Cameron Eric Leon, Max Hardswell, MaXx Decco, Michael Christian, Mike Oxready, Miles Long, Mr-Charlie Smith, Nanette D'angelo Sylvan, Nolan Neptune, Orion Blaze Browne, Owlejandro Monroe, Papa Cherry, Papi Chulo, Papi Chulo Doll, Persian Prince, Phantom, Pierce Gabriel, Rasta Boi Punany, Rico M Taylor, Rock McGroyn, Rocky Valentino, Rogue DRAG King, Romeo Sanchez, Rychard "Alpha" Le'Sabre, Ryder Knightly, Ryder Long, Sam Masterson, Sammy Silver, Santana Romero, Scorpio, Shane Rebel Caine, Shook ByNature, Silk Steele Prince, SirMandingo Thatis, Smitty O'Toole, Soco Dupree, Spacee Kadett, Starr Masters, Stefan LeDude, Stefon Royce Iman, Stefon SanDiego, Stormm, Teddy Michael, Thug Passion, Travis Luvermore, Travis Hard, Trey C. Michaels, Trigger Montgomery, Tyler Manhattan, Viciouse Slick, Vinnie Marconi, Welland Dowd, William Vanity Matrix, Wulf Von Monroe, Xander Havoc, and Xavier Bottoms.

Book 5:   DRAG411's
"DRAG Stories"

Funny stories shared with Todd Kachinski Kottmeier including the following contributors of DRAG Stories to include Chance Wise, Anson Reign, Tiffani Middlesexx, Rico Taylor, Todd Kachinski Kottmeier, Bob Taylor, Stefon Royce Iman, Candi Samples, Alexis Mateo, Naomi Wynters, Dmentia Divinyl, Bruce Lacie, Kennedy Wendy, Chastity Rose, Miss GiGi, Angel gLamar, Patricia Grand, Shook ByNature, Lady Guy, Eunyce Raye, Charley Marie Coutora, Jezzie Bell, Lamar Kellam, Jayden St. James, Rachelle Ann Summers, Champagne T Bordeaux, Gilda Golden, Daisha Monet, Vivika D'Angelo, Rachel Boheme, Esme Rodriguez, and MaNu Da Original.

Book 6:   DRAG411's
"DRAG Mother, DRAG Father" Honoring Mentors

Performers look to DRAG mothers, DRAG fathers, friends, and fans for insight, compassion, and guidance as mentors. This book honors those special people. Over 140 entertainers contributed wisdom and words for this historical book, making it the largest project of its nature in GLBTQ history and the first published book on male and female mentors.

Commentary shared with Todd Kachinski Kottmeier included the following contributors of DRAG Parents to includee AJ Menendez, Vinnie Marconi, Mis Sadistic, Todd Kachinski Kottmeier, Bob Taylor, Taina Norell, Andrew Stratton, Horchata Horchata, David Warner, Gianna Love, Trinity Taylor, Domunique Jazmin Vizcaya, Brittany Moore, PurrZsa Kyttyn, Jake Lickus, Shelita Taylor, Adriana Manchez, MiMi Welch, China Taylor, Armondis Bone't, Monique Trudeau, Simeon Codfish, Diamond Dupree, Stefon Royce Iman, Jayden Stjames, Demonica da Bomb, Colin Grey, Christopher Todd Guy, Celyndra Lashay Clyne, Candice St. James, Justin Barnes Williams, Ivanna Dooche, London Taylor Douglas, Christina Alexandria Victoria Regina Lowe, Bianca DeMonet, Critiqa Mann, Jazmen Andrews, AJ Allen, TotiYanah Diamond, D' Marco Knight, Chip Matthews, Mirage Montrese, India Starr Simms, Jade S Stratton, Emerald Divine, Elysse Giovanni, Vanity Halston, Kristofer Reynolds, Akasha Uravitch, Adriana Fuentes, Erykah Mirage, Felicity Ferraro, Joey Payge, Rhiannon Todd, Vicious Slick, Amirage Saling, Tori Sass, Chy'enne Valentino, and Robbi Lynn.

Book 7:   DRAG411's
"Spotlight Today"

It was the World's Largest Paperback Magazine for Impersonators and Fans when it premiered with over
175 pages. DRAG411 no longer prints Spotlight Today Magazine, but here is the re-release of the groundbreaking first edition. Complete articles by Vinnie Marconi, Denise Russell, Tiffani T. Middlesexx, Kristofer Reynolds, Magenta Alexandria Dupree, Butch Daddy, Vivikah Kayson-Raye, Makanoe, Amanda Lay, Thomas DeVoyd, Kevin B. Reed, Glenn Storm, and over 150 impersonators from around the world.

Book 8:   DRAG411's
"DRAG Queen Guide"

Almost two hundred female impersonators around the world share over a thousand insightful comments in forty-one chapters.
Commentary shared with Todd Kachinski Kottmeier included the following contributors of Official DRAG Queen and Female Impersonator Handbook to include Alana Summers, Alexis Marie Von Furstenburg, Alize', Aloe Vera, Alysin Wonderland, Amanda Bone DeMornay, Amanda Lay, Amanda Roberts, Amy DeMilo, Anastasia Fallon, Angie Ovahness, Anita Mandinite, Appolonia Cruz, Ashlyn Tyler, Aurora Tr'Nele Michelle, Azia Sparks, Barbie Dayne, Barbra Herr, Beverly LaSalle, Bianca DeMonet, Bianca Lynn Breeze, Blair Michaels, Boxxa Vine, Brittany T Moore, Britney Towers, Brandi Amara Skyy, Brooke Lynn Bradshaw, Candi Samples, Candi Stratton, Candy Sugar, Cathy Craig, Catia Lee Love, CeCe Georgia, Cee-Cee LaRouge-Avalon, Celeste Starr, Chad Michaels, Chevon Davis, Cheyenne Desoto Mykels, Chi Chi Lalique, Christina Collins, Chrystal Conners, Claudia B Eautiful, Coca Mesa, Coco St James, Damiana LaRoux, Dana Scrumptious, Danyel Vasquez, Dee Gregory, Delores T. Van-Cartier, Demonica DaBaum, Denise Russell, Diamond Dunhill, Diva Lilo, Diva Savage, Dove, EdriAna Treviño, Elle Emenopé, Elysse Giovanni, Erica James, Esmé Rodríguez, Estella Sweet, Eunyce Raye, Eva Nichole Distruction, Faleasha Savage, Felicia Minor, Felicity Frockaccino, Gigi Masters, Ginger Alley, Ginger Gigi Diamond, Ginger Kaye Belmont, Glitz Glam, Grecia Montes D' Occa, Heather Daniels, Hennessy Heart, Hershae Chocolatae, Holy McGrail, Hope B Childs, Horchata, India Brooks, India Ferrah, Ivy Profen, Izzy Adahl, Jaclyn St James, Jade Iroq, Jade Sotomayor, Jade Taylor Stratton, Jamie-Ree Swan, Jennifer Warner, Jessica Brooks, Jexa Ren'ae Van de Kamp, Joey Brooks, Jonny Pride, Kamelle Toe, Karma Jayde Addams, Kelly Turner, Mama Savannah Georgia, Mr. Kenneth Blake, Kamden T. Rage, Kira Stone-St James, Kirby Kolby, Kita Rose, Krysta Radiance, Lacie Bruce, Lady Jasmine Michaels, Lady Pearl, Lady Sabrina, Latrice Royale, LaTonga Manchez, Leona Barr, Lexi Alexander, Lilo Monroe, Lindsay Carlton, Lucinda Holliday, Lunara Sky, Lupita Chiquita Michaels Alexander, Madam Diva Divine, Mahog Anny, Makayla Michelle Davis Diamond, Mariah Cherry, Maxine Padlock, Melody Mayheim, Menaje E'toi, Mercede Andrews, Mi$hal, Mia Fierce, Michelle Leigh Sterling, Miss Diva Savage, Miss GiGi, Misty Eyez, Mitze Peterbilt, Monica Mystique, Montrese Lamar Hollar, Morgana DeRaven, Muffy Vanbeaverhousen, Natasha Richards, Nathan Loveland, Nicole Paige Brooks, Nikki Garcia, Nostalgia Todd Ronin, Olivia St James, Paige Sinclair, Pandora DeCeption, Pheobe James, Reia'Cheille Lucious, Robyn Demornay, Robyn Graves, Rhonda Sheer, Rose Murphy, Ruby Diamond NY, Ruby Holiday, Ryan Royale, Rychard "Alpha" Le'Sabre, Rye Seronie,

Sable Monay, Sabrina Kayson-Raye, Samantha St Clair, Sanaa Raelynn, Sapphire T. Mylan, Sasha Phillips, Savannah Rivers, Savannah Stevens, Selina Kyle, Sha'day Halston-St James, ShaeShae LaReese, Shamya Banx, Shana Nicole, Shaunna Rai, Sierra Foxx White, Sierra Santana, Sonja Jae Savage, Stella D'oro, Strawberry Whip, Sugarpill, Tasha Carter, Tanna Blake, Taquella Roze, Tawdri Hipburn, Taylor Rockland, Tempest DuJour, Tiffani T. Middlesexx, Traci Russell, Trudy Tyler, Vanessa del Rey, Velveeta WhoreMel, Vera Delmar, Vicky Summers, Vita DeVine, Vivian Sorensin, Vivian Von Brokenhymen, Vivika D'Angelo-Steele, Wendy G. Kennedy, Willmuh Dickfit, Wynter Storm, Yasmine Alexander and ZuZu Bella.

Book 9:   DRAG411's (Two Comedy Scripts)
"Best Said Dead" and **"Following Wynter"**

Best Said Dead examines in funny conversations those brief minutes after a person dies. Many religions and beliefs define different paths for each of us. Rarely do we discuss those precious moments between death and the final destination. This comedy opens the possibilities that for a moment, a person vanishes into the memories in their mind. Any part can be male, female, or ambiguous.

Following Wynter is a hilarious comedy play. Ethan discovers his newlywed husband is the flamboyant DRAG queen Wynter Storm in this whimsical farce with an important message of believing in yourself and your friends. . . even if your friend is Serena Silver. Any part can be male, female, or ambiguous.

Book 10:   DRAG411's
"DRAG World"
The contributing writers of DRAG411's "Spotlight Magazine," the World's Largest Paperback Magazine for Impersonators and Fans when it premiered in 2012 with over 175 pages, created this companion book. DRAG411 no longer prints Spotlight Today Magazine, but above you will find Book 7 is the re-release of the groundbreaking first edition. Complete chapters on DRAG Marketing by DRAG411.
Complimentary articles on Confidence, Duct Tape, Music Selection, Living Divinely, authentic stage presence, Pageants, having fun performing, jewelry, legislative information from the United States and around the world, the Old School performers, Virgin stage performers, and payday from contributing writers including Denise Russell, Jay Santana, Chance Wise, Vivikah Kayson-Raye, AJ Menedez, Glenn Storm, Freddy Prinze Charming, Gage Gatlyn, Kevin B. Reed, and over 100 impersonators from around the world!

**Other books from the Best Selling author
The Infamous Todd Kachinski Kottmeier**

Other books from the Best Selling author
The Infamous Todd Kachinski Kottmeier

"Turn Around Bright Eyes, The DRAG Queen Killer"

Few crimes in gay history rocked a nation as great as The DRAG Queen Killer. The country seemed paralyzed from the first ring of the chain tapping on the concrete, as they pulled Cassandra to her death, until the very last brutal killing. The murderous rampage seemed buried amongst the media suffering from a barrage of tales from the 9-11 terrorist attacks.

"CommUnity of Transition"

We sent over a thousand invitations to the transgender community around the world asking them to share wisdom, advice, and compassion for those questioning or struggling. No restraints, using topics they created, as they guided the conversation over forty chapters and fifty topics. By the close, these remarkable people had created the largest compilation book in transgender history. They opened their heart with these words.

NOTE: *This book is "lightly edited" to reflect the intent and form of over one hundred transgender contributors. Unedited photographs "before and after" come from actual contributing transgender writers.*

"Joey Brooks, The Show Must Go On"

By Joey Brooks and Todd Kachinski Kottmeier

Joey Brooks, The Show Must Go On is the story of The First Lady of Ybor from the days of El Goya to present day. Female Impersonator, Show director, hostess, author...

"Old school, new school, no school... who gives a shit? I'm too old to go to school. I barely remember last week. When I get too old to remember what the fuck I did when I was young ...ger, I'll just open one of these books and laugh my ass off. I wonder how many other queens had this much fun becoming one of the icons of their community. Too funny. I just called myself an icon. Hell, I must be a queen. Only a female impersonator could call themselves a diva, a queen, a star without people giggling behind her back. Giggling is good. A twenty-dollar bill is better."

"Two Days Past Dead"

The Author's First Published Book

It is hard to be the good guy when you succeed so well being bad. This is the Auggie Summer's dilemma his entire life. The story, based loosely on the tales of The Infamous Todd, follows the precocious child. His story begins with selling candy in 9th grade where he catches not only the attention of the press but also amusement of the drug cartel early in its' own infancy. Auggie Summers finds himself in the forefront of one of the most dangerous organizations on Earth.

"Waiting On God"

The Author's Humorist Novel

Learn to live after the doctors tell you "that are dying." A humorist essay on embracing funny moments and to create an environment around you that makes people not only laugh, but also be inspired by your strength.